1-2-3 Calligraphy!

Letters and Projects for Beginners and Beyond

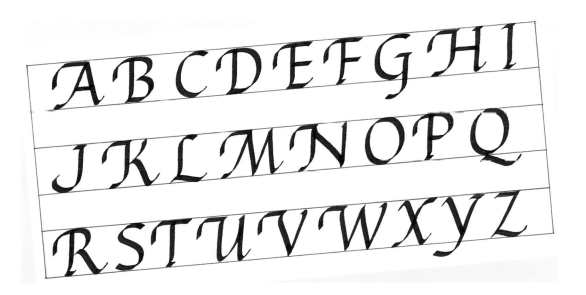

Eleanor Winters

UNION
SQUARE
kids

NEW YORK

For Margaret and Dolores
and of course for you, Leendert, with all my love

Acknowledgments

Thank you to all who have advised and assisted in the process of creating *1–2–3 Calligraphy!* Extra special thanks goes to Carole Maurer, my partner and pal, who always knows how to get the job done; to Joan Harmon for pages and pages of perfect guide lines; and to Julia Paterson, friend and advisor from day one. I am also grateful to Kathy Wallace for her calligraphic envelopes and to Lisa Flynn for her fine photography. To the editorial and production staff at Sterling, especially Heather Quinlan and Jeanette Green: many, many thanks; I could not have done this without you.

UNION
SQUARE
kids

NEW YORK

UNION SQUARE KIDS and the distinctive Union Square Kids logo are registered trademarks of Union Square & Co., LLC.

Union Square & Co., LLC., is a subsidiary of Sterling Publishing Co., Inc.

ISBN 978-1-4549-3652-7

For information about custom editions, special sales, and premium purchases, please contact specialsales@unionsquareandco.com.

Printed in China

Lot #:
4 6 8 10 9 7 5 3
12/22

unionsquareandco.com

Contents

Introduction

welcome!

We hope that kids who are already hooked on calligraphy as well as kids eager to begin will enjoy this book.

If you've already tried some calligraphy alphabets, you are probably ready for more. Calligraphy, as you already know, opens many new doors and invites you to explore a wonderful world of shapes and colors and techniques.

If this book is your first experience with calligraphy, you've come to the right place! Chapters 1, 2, and 3 review some of the basics of lettering and the art materials you will be using. The instructions in the later chapters will be easy to follow if you spend some time doing the exercises and practicing the techniques in these first chapters.

For those of you already familiar with calligraphy, it's still worth taking a look at the opening chapters, especially if you haven't picked up your calligraphy pens lately.

1–2–3 Calligraphy offers something for everyone: new ways to do "old" alphabets and some other alphabets you are probably seeing for the first time. Plus it presents projects and techniques that give you many new ways to use your calligraphy, such as making signs, designing stationery, addressing colorful envelopes, making calligrams (calligraphic pictures), and more.

This book even looks into some of the basic rules and steps of layout and design so that you can make calligraphy art, such as poems or quotations to hang on the wall.

Who knows? This could be the beginning—or the continuation—of a lifelong interest.

PART I

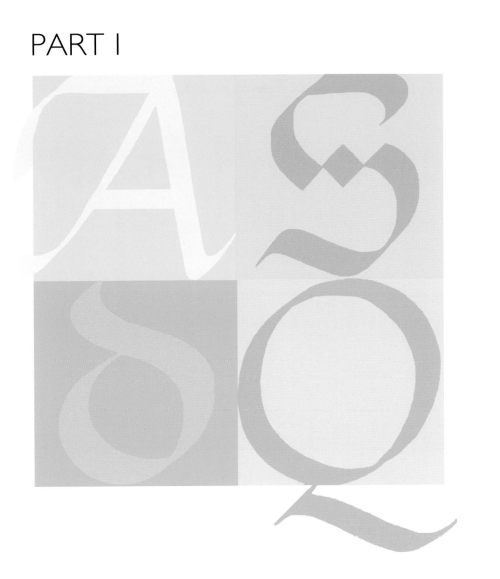

LET'S BEGIN

Back to the Basics

A **word to the wise:** Read this chapter even if you are already doing calligraphy. It may remind you of some things you have forgotten or teach you some things you should know.

In this chapter we look at the basic tools you'll need and the rules you should follow. Let's begin with your art materials.

PENS

When you first learn lettering, you generally write or draw the letters with a pencil, or perhaps a pointed marker. This gives you an idea of the "skeleton" of the alphabet: the basic bones of the letters, without any thick or thin lines.

The instructions and examples in this book call mostly for calligraphy markers. These may be markers made by Zig, Itoya, Y & C, or other felt-tipped calligraphy pens that make thick and thin lines. They all look pretty much like those in the photo below.

We'll skip over pencils and pointed markers and start right in with calligraphy markers, because these are colorful and make more beautiful, interesting letters than pointed markers. However, pointed markers will be useful in learning Italic handwriting in Chapter 9. Because calligraphy markers demand a little more skill than normal pens, we'll give you some pen position warm-up exercises in Chapter 3.

Fountain pens are also fun to use for calligraphy. Try calligraphy fountain pens with broad (B-3 or B) and medium (B-2 or M) nibs. You'll find several brands to choose from. Get some ink cartridges to fit the fountain pens as well. Be sure that the cartridges are made for your pen; not all ink cartridges fit all pens.

PAPER

White practice paper is easy to find. You can use copy machine paper or buy a pad of layout paper at an art shop. Be sure to use paper that's thin enough so that you can see your guide lines through it. You can check the paper by placing a sheet of it over one of the guide line pages found in the back of this book. If you can see the guide lines easily, your paper is the right thickness (or thinness) for practicing. Don't use tracing paper because it doesn't have a nice surface to write on.

Some kinds of papers "bleed," which means that they absorb the ink. If this happens, your writing will look fuzzy. Test your paper by writing a line or a letter on it with your fountain pen. If the paper bleeds, try another kind of paper.

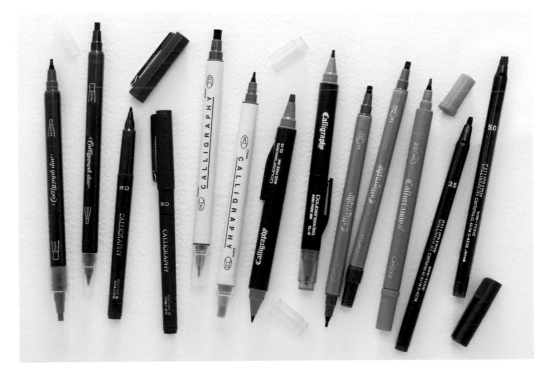

Calligraphy markers.

OTHER MATERIALS

You'll need some other art materials a little later (for a few projects in Part III), but for now you are all set to begin. Remember that guide lines appear in the back of this book; more will be said about them later.

If you've already been doing calligraphy, then you've learned how to sit, how to hold your pens, the best light to use, etc. Rather than repeating all of that, here are a few main points.

THINGS TO REMEMBER

1. Sit up straight with your feet on the floor. Don't do calligraphy lying down or with your head resting on the table.

2. Use good light so you can see what you are doing. If you are right-handed, the light should be either in front of you or coming from the left side. If you are left-handed, it should be in front of you or coming from the right side.

3. Keep your paper clean by leaning on a "guard sheet," a piece of paper placed over the writing surface just below the line you are writing on. Try not to put your hands directly on the paper on which you are writing.

4. Keep your paper tilted slightly uphill to the right if you are right-handed, or downhill to the right, if you are left-handed.

5. **Advice to lefties:** There are special fountain pens for left-handed people with the nib (pen point) slanted slightly to the left to make writing easier. Unfortunately, there aren't left-handed markers, at least not yet. You'll need to find a comfortable position so that you can write with your hand *under the writing line, rather than above.* If you keep your left elbow close to your waist, it will be easier to hold your pen in the proper position.

Try adjusting the slant of your paper, with the right edge pointing downhill, until you are comfortable and the pen is in the correct position relative to the writing line. See the illustrations in Chapter 3, page 12.

6. Don't forget to PRACTICE! Even if you've been doing calligraphy for a long time, it always helps to exercise. Find some time every day, or at least twice a week, to work on your calligraphy. The more you practice, the easier it will be and the faster you'll learn. And of course, you'll have much more fun.

2

Calligraphy Vocabulary

Here's a quick review of the calligraphic terms that we'll use. The most important word is *calligraphy,* which means beautiful writing.

There are many different styles of calligraphy, which are called **hands,** as in "the Italic hand" or "the Roman hand." Most hands have **minuscules** (lowercase letters) and **capitals,** although there are some hands that consist of only lowercase letters or only capitals.

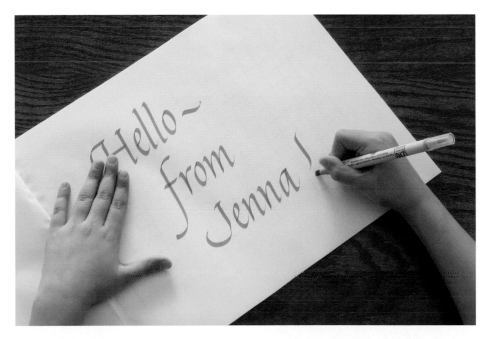

Following are a few more terms frequently used in calligraphy.

THE PARTS OF THE LETTERS

ascender   the upper part of the lowercase (minuscule) letters that extends above the waistline (for example, the top of the **b, h,** and **k**)

ascender line   the guide line that marks the top of the minuscule letters with ascenders. The top of the **b, h,** and **k** will touch the ascender line.

baseline   the line on which most letters "sit." All lowercase letters rest on the baseline, except those with descenders.

descender   the lower part of the minuscule letters that extends below the baseline (for example, the bottom of the **g, j,** and **y**)

descender line   the guide line that marks the bottom of the minuscule letters with descenders. The bottom of the **g, j,** and **y** will touch the descender line.

waistline   the line that marks the top of the **x**-height space

x-height   the height of the lowercase **x** and of all the small lowercase letters (like the **a, c,** and **e**); also the top part of the letters that have descenders and the bottom part of letters that have ascenders.

MORE CALLIGRAPHIC VOCABULARY

counter   the inside of the letter (for example, the part of the **o** enclosed by the pen line)

cross-stroke   a horizontal stroke from left to right, such as the stroke used to cross the **t** or the **f**

entrance stroke   the small stroke with which many letters begin

exit stroke   the small stroke with which many letters end

guard sheet   a piece of paper used to protect the paper you are writing on. Your hand will rest on the guard sheet when you write.

guide lines   the lines that you either draw on your paper or put under your paper (seen through another sheet of paper) to help you make your letters the correct height

hairline   the thinnest stroke your pen can make

nib   the pen point

pen angle or pen position   the relationship between the edge of the nib and the baseline (see Chapter 3, "Pens and Pen Positions")

spacing   the space between letters in a word

stroke   any mark or line made with your pen

3

Pens and Pen Positions

PENS

Most of the calligraphy in this book was written with either fountain pens or colored markers, the markers that are made especially for what we call *broad-edged pen calligraphy*. These are sometimes called chisel-edged markers. You'll work mostly with 3.5-millimeter (3.5-mm) width marker nibs, which give you a medium-size line, like this.

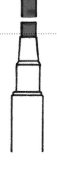

When you change nib sizes, you'll use some markers that are wider, measuring 5 mm, and some that are narrower. The narrower ones are 2-mm markers.

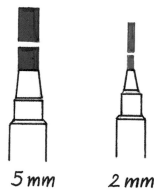

5 mm   *2 mm*

Here's a basic rule

The size (height) of your letter depends on the width of your pen nib. A wider nib gives you a taller letter, and a narrower nib gives you a shorter letter.

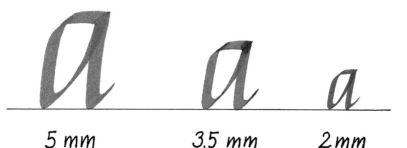

| 5 mm | 3.5 mm | 2mm |

When practicing with fountain pens, you will also have the opportunity to try writing letters that are different heights. You will probably find fountain pens just as easy to use as markers. Since it's usually easier to get an extra-wide marker than a similarly wide fountain pen, when you learn to write large (Chapter 14), you'll use markers. Otherwise, you can decide which kinds of pens you prefer.

The guide lines on pages 115–127 were made to fit the nibs (markers and fountain pens) that you'll be using. Be sure to use the correct lines for each alphabet and pen size. It's a good idea to make photocopies of each of the guide line pages, so that they can be placed under the sheet of white paper that

you'll be writing on. If you make copies of all the guide lines in advance, you'll have them ready for the alphabet you are learning and the pen you choose.

PEN POSITIONS

If you have already studied calligraphy, you probably know something about *pen position* or *pen angle*. These terms describe the relationship between the edge of your nib (or pen point) and the baseline (the line you are writing on).

Here are examples of how to hold your pen in two different pen positions: the **diagonal** pen position—or **45-degree** pen angle—and the **flattened** pen position—or **30-degree** pen angle.

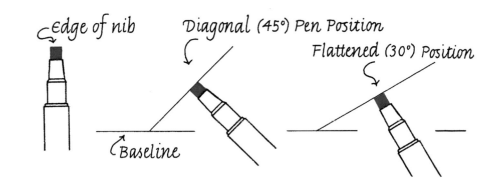

Edge of nib   Diagonal (45°) Pen Position

Flattened (30°) Position

Baseline

The thickness and thinness of the strokes (lines) you make depends on the pen position and the direction of the stroke—which way you move the pen.

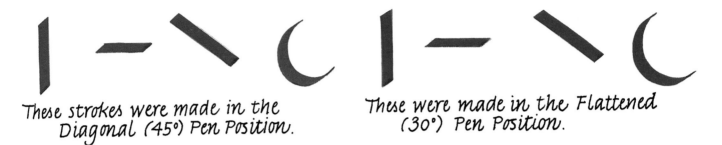

These strokes were made in the Diagonal (45°) Pen Position.

These were made in the Flattened (30°) Pen Position.

Spend a little time doing some exercises to get your pen in the correct writing positions. Zigzags help you keep your pen in one position without changing it. When you make crosses in the diagonal pen position, the two lines should be equal in thickness. Crosses made in the flattened position have a heavier downstroke and a thinner cross-stroke.

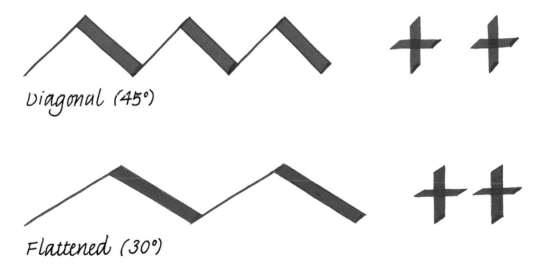

Diagonal (45°)

Flattened (30°)

Some alphabets, such as Italic and Gothic, call for the diagonal (45-degree) pen position, while others use the flattened pen position. Although there are other alphabets written with still more pen positions, let's limit ourselves to two ways of holding the pen: the diagonal and the flattened positions.

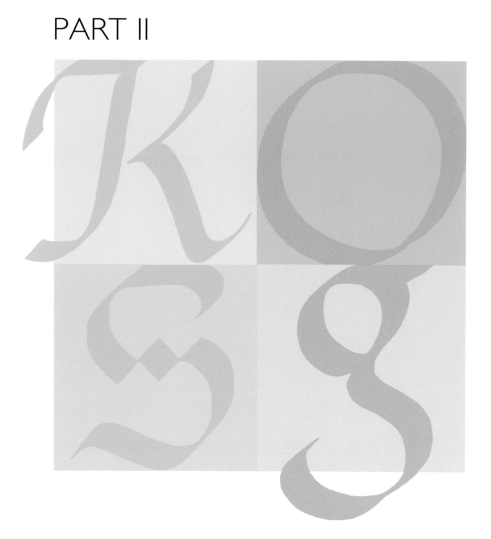

PART II

The ALPHABETS

4

Italic

A Quick Review

BASIC ITALIC

The Italic alphabet is one of the most popular and useful styles of calligraphy. The minuscule letters are made with your pen in the 45-degree (diagonal) position and slant slightly to the right. The letters on the next few pages were written with a 3.5-mm marker (see pages 15–18).

Notice that the three parts of the letters—the ascender, x-height, and descender—are all of equal length, and that the alphabet is rather narrow.

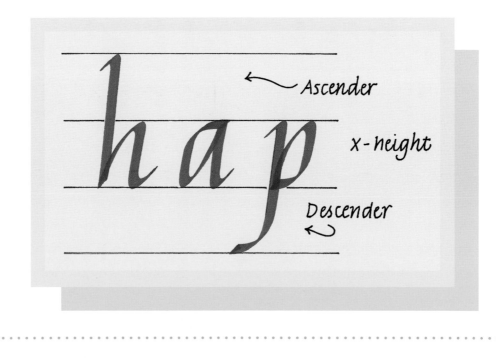

Here is the Italic alphabet.

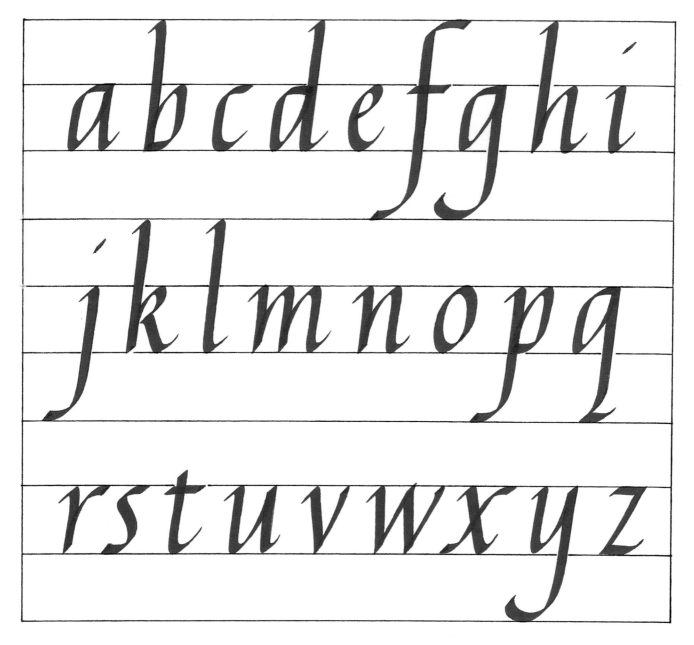

You can try these letters (or review them if you've already learned them) using Guide Lines #1, which you'll find on page 115.

If this is your first experience with Italic, try practicing the letters in groups, starting with the simplest letters. Use the following chart so that you know which way to move your pen (left, right, up, down, etc.). All the letters can be made in a single stroke (without lifting the pen) with the exception of **d, e, f, p, t,** and **x.**

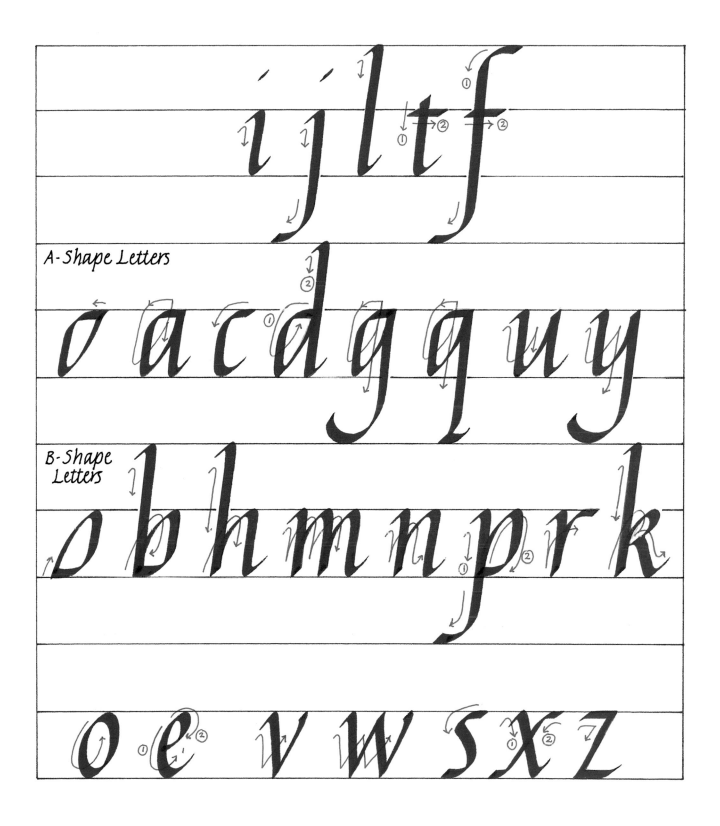

A-Shape Letters

B-Shape Letters

THINGS TO REMEMBER

1. All the Italic letters are made with your pen in the diagonal pen position. Look what happens if your pen is held differently.

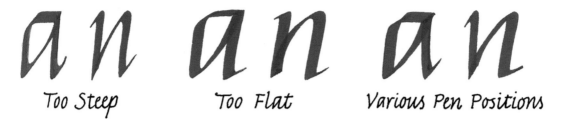

Too Steep   Too Flat   Various Pen Positions

2. Be sure to make all of these letters the same width: **a, b, d, g, h, n, p, q, u,** and **y.** They are all based on either the **a-shape** or the **b-shape.**

3. Try to make the entrance and exit strokes (the beginnings and endings of the letters) carefully. If you turn your paper upside down, they should look the same as they do right side up. These strokes look like this.

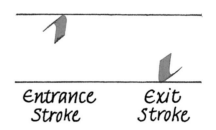

Entrance   Exit
Stroke   Stroke

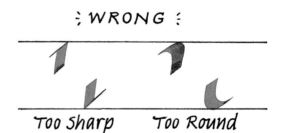

⁝ WRONG ⁝

Too Sharp   Too Round

4. Write slowly! That way, you will make the nicest possible letters. Here are some tricky words to practice. They were written with a fountain pen. You can try these with a B or B-3 fountain pen, using Guide Lines #2 on page 116.

flattery calligraphy

gypsy banana cherry

zigzag wallboard

5. Spacing is important! The basic spacing rule for Italic and for all other calligraphy is this:

*When making words, the space **between** the letters should appear to be about the same as the space **inside** the letters.*

5

More Italic

Some New Letters

ITALIC VARIATIONS

Once you are familiar with Italic minuscules, you can begin to add some letter variations to your basic A-B-C.

Here's a new way to make the tops (ascenders) of the taller letters. This stroke looks the same as the top and left side of the letter **a.** It is a variation on the ascender of the **b, d, h, k,** and **l.**

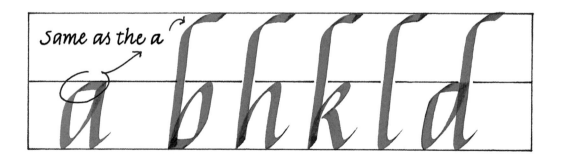

You can also vary the descenders of the **g** and **y**, making them a little more decorative.

This new shape, which we call a **teardrop descender,** can be done in one or two strokes.

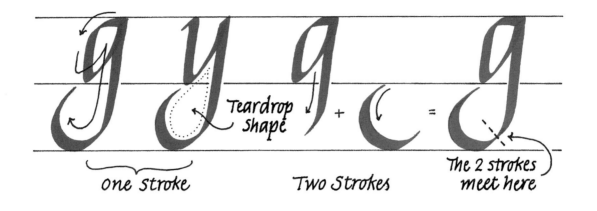

one stroke　　Two Strokes　　The 2 strokes meet here

Teardrop Shape

And here are a few more variations on the Italic minuscules.

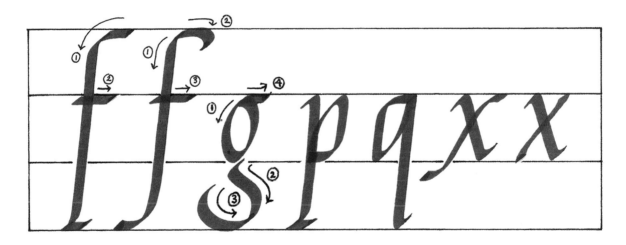

Varying the Proportions

All the letters we just showed you were done with the normal proportions, that is, with equal length ascenders, x-heights, and descenders.

You can also change the way your letters appear by either shortening or lengthening the ascenders and descenders, without changing the size of the x-height. In the case of shortened ascenders and descenders (below), notice that the letters look a little simpler than the basic Italic alphabet. You can try these using Guide Lines #3 on page 117.

Shortened Ascenders

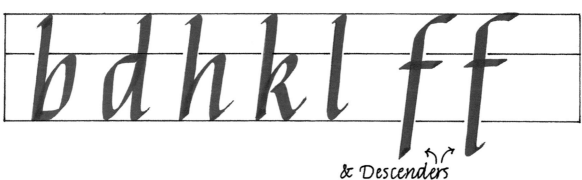

& Descenders

Shortened Descenders

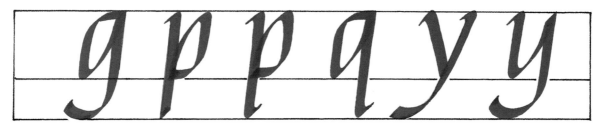

Try writing a short text using these simplified letters. You will probably see that the second example below looks more textured than the first one, which has longer ascenders and descenders. The closer the lines are together, the less white space there is between lines and the more textured or dense the writing appears.

Here's an example of a sentence written both ways—first with the normal proportions and then with the new proportions (on Guide Lines #5A).

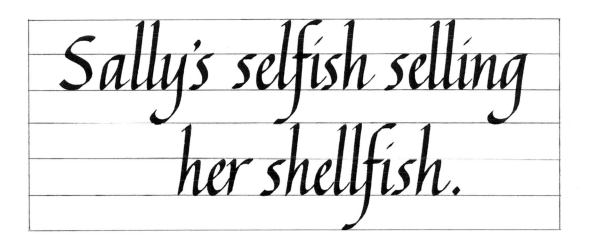

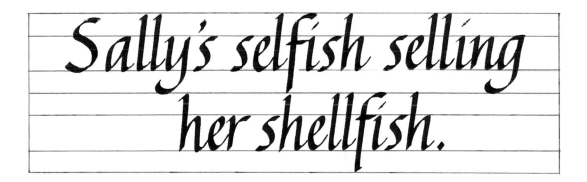

The previous example was written with a fountain pen with a broad nib so it would fit in this book. If you use your 3.5-mm marker, you will get the same effect, but you will need to write on a larger piece of paper.

You can also make longer ascenders and descenders. If you do that, your letters will look a little more decorative, or **flourished.** Try some of the following styles, using Guide Lines #4 on page 118. These lines allow some extra space for the ascenders and descenders. Be sure that you use the smaller space for your x-height. There's a little "x" printed on the baselines to help you write in the correct spaces.

Here are some decorative ascender and descender letters. When you make the tops of your letters more flourished, it's usually easier to do them in two strokes, as shown here.

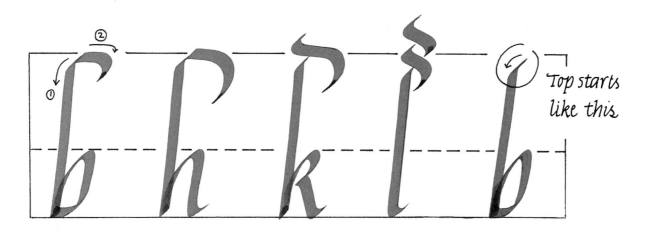

Top starts like this

If you'd like to try writing a text with the smaller marker (2 mm) or the wide fountain pen (B or B-3), use Guide Lines #5A on page 119. The extra space for the ascenders and descenders in Guide lines #5B, also on page 119, will allow you to try some decorative letters.

The example below was written with a 2-mm marker, using the proportions explained above—the standard size x-height and the longer ascenders and descenders.

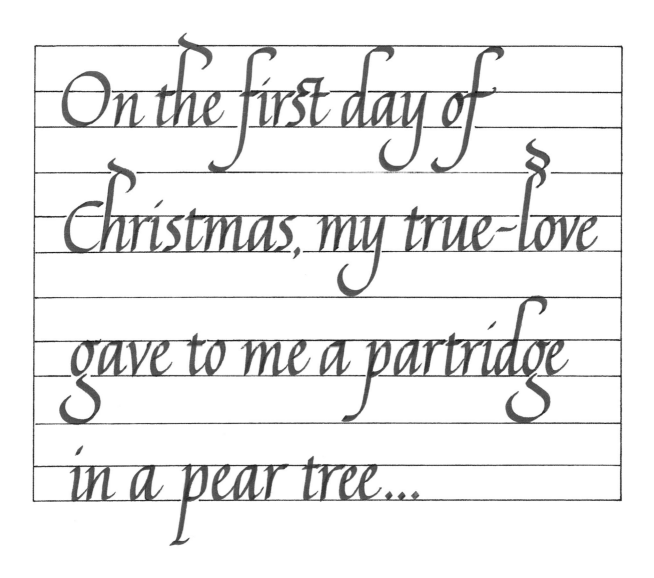

Speaking of flourishes, you can add decorative endings to the **r, s, f,** and **t,** like this.

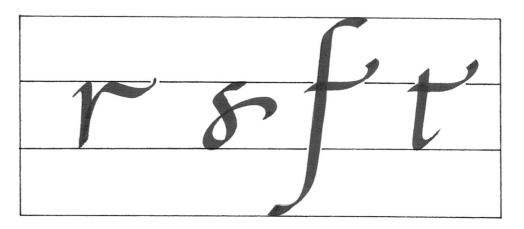

Just be sure to use these endings only at the end of a word, never in the middle.

YES:

for but of yes

NO:

ask often boring

6

A Brief Pause for a Math Lesson

*B*efore going any further, let's stop to learn a new and important fact.

The x-height of Italic minuscules is five times the width of the edge of the pen.

Or to put it another way: *x-height = 5 pen widths*

A look at the mathematics behind calligraphy will help you understand why particular guide lines are used when working with pens or markers of certain sizes.

But don't panic! If this arithmetic is still a year or two beyond what you are doing in school, just skip this chapter and come back to it when you are ready. Just keep in mind that it really is important to learn sooner or later.

Here's how it works: Your calligraphy nib—whether a marker or another kind of pen—has a certain measurement along the edge. The illustration below shows how a 3.5-mm nib and a 2-mm nib are measured. Your broad, or B-3, fountain pen also measures approximately 2 mm.

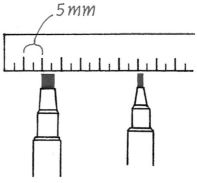
5 mm

For those who measure in inches, 3.5 millimeters equals about ⅛ inch, but since markers are labeled in metric measurements, this explanation will use millimeters. The abbreviation for millimeters is *mm.*

The height of a lowercase (minuscule) letter generally means the x-height—the height of the letter **x** and of all the other minuscule letters without ascenders or descenders. The term *x-height* also applies to the lower half of letters that have an ascender and the upper half of letters that have a descender.

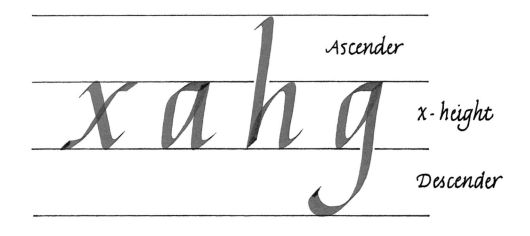

Now, back to the math. If the x-height for Italic letters is five times the width of the nib, then a letter made with a nib that measures 2 mm would have an x-height of 10 mm (5 × 2 mm = 10 mm). And if the nib measures 3.5 mm, the x-height would be 5 × 3.5, which equals 17.5 mm.

These measurements can be made *visually,* as well as mathematically. Hold your pen so that the edge of the nib is parallel to the sides of your paper. Then make little marks by moving the pen to the right. When you make five of these little marks, one above the other, like steps, the distance from the top of the top mark to the bottom of the bottom mark is equal to five pen widths.

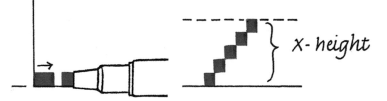

Using this "step" method, you can figure out how far apart to make your guide lines for any alphabet, using any pen, even if you don't know how many millimeters the pen measures.

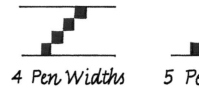 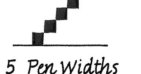 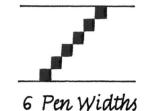

4 Pen Widths   5 Pen Widths   6 Pen Widths

Making these little measurement drawings (steps) is sometimes easier than doing the math, but it's good to understand the mathematics behind calligraphy.

The guide lines in this book are drawn so that the spaces for the letters will be *mathematically correct* for the pens you are using. If you measure the space between lines on your basic Italic Guide Lines (#1) using a metric ruler, you will see that it measures exactly 17.5 mm. And since the ascender, x-height, and descender for basic Italic are all the same size, all the spaces on this page are 17.5 mm.

This is probably more mathematics than you ever bargained for. But it will help you understand what happens when, in the next chapter, you experiment with breaking the rules.

7

Back to Italic

Changing the Weight of the Letters

The **weight** of the letter means the thickness of the strokes that form it. You might also say that it is the proportion of the black lines (the calligraphy) to the white space. Let's compare heavyweight letters with lightweight letters.

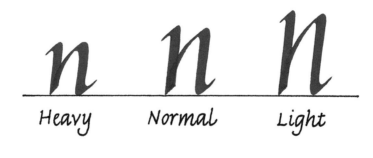

Heavy   Normal   Light

HEAVIER-WEIGHT LETTERS

In order to make heavier letters, you can write Italic letters in a space that is shorter than normal. For example, these **a**'s were made with a 3.5-mm marker, first in a normal space (measuring 5 pen widths or 17.5 mm), then between lines that are closer together.

As you can see, when you use the same pen in a shorter space, the letters will look thicker and heavier. Even a small difference in the height of the letter can make a big difference in the weight.

The Italic letters below were written with all the spaces shorter than the usual five-pen-width space. All the parts of the letters—the ascenders, x-height, and descenders—are equal to each other.

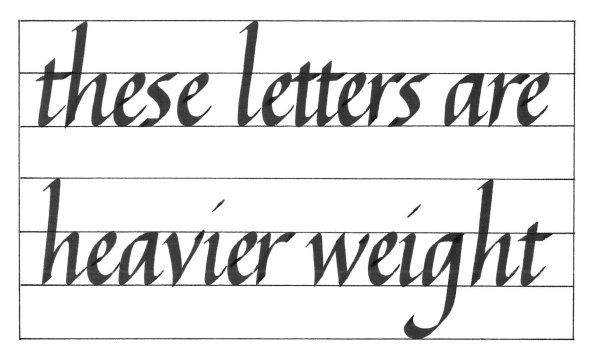

Try experimenting with shorter (heavier) letters by using a 3.5-mm marker on Guide Lines #6 on page 120. These guide lines measure four times the width of the nib instead of five, so you'll have less space in which to fit your letters. If the space is even smaller, the letters will look even thicker, like this.

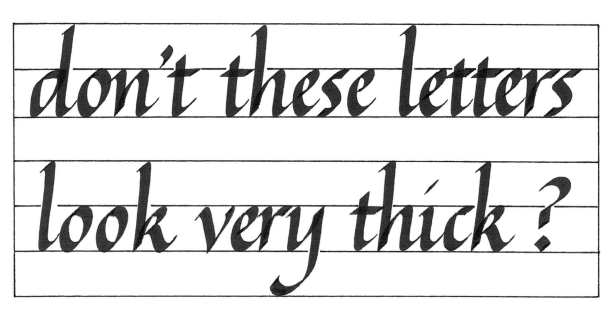

LIGHTER-WEIGHT LETTERS

With more space in which to write Italic letters, rather than less space, the letters will appear to be thinner, or lighter weight. In the examples below, the space between the lines measures six and then seven pen widths, rather than the five pen widths of standard Italic.

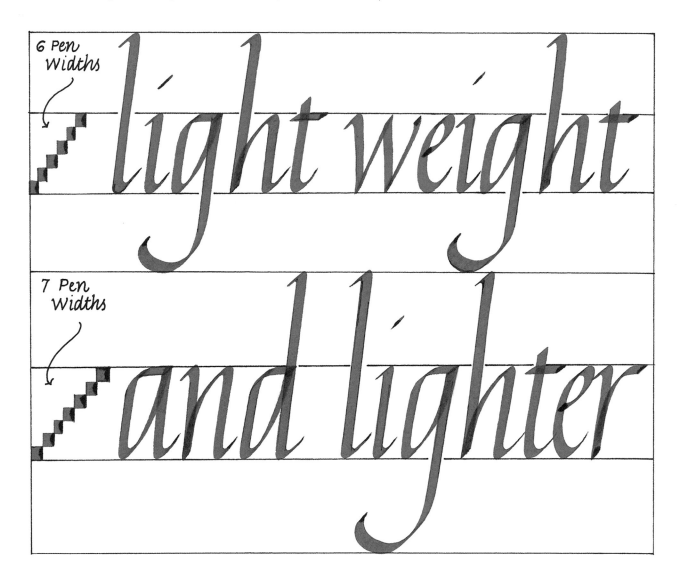

When you have extra space for the ascenders, try making some of the flourished letters, like this.

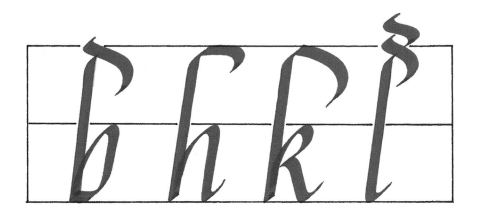

However, it is not such a good idea to use the decorative tops (ascenders) when the space is shortened. This looks a little crowded, doesn't it?

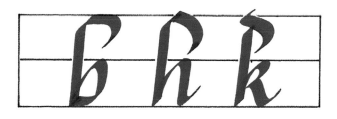

Try these new letters using a 3.5-mm marker and Guide Lines #7 (see page 120), which will give you extra height for your Italic letters. See which style you prefer: normal-size letters that measure five pen widths; taller, thinner letters (six pen widths); or shorter, thicker letters (four pen widths).

As an exercise, try writing the same text or quotation three times to compare the different weights. Use some of the Italic letter variations from Chapter 5.

On page 34 there's some sample text you can copy. This was written with a fountain pen. The height of the first two lines is five pen widths; the next two are six pen widths; and the last two are four pen widths.

To try the heavier-weight letters with your fountain pen or 2-mm marker, use Guide Lines #8A; for lighter-weight letters, use Guide Lines #8B (see page 121).

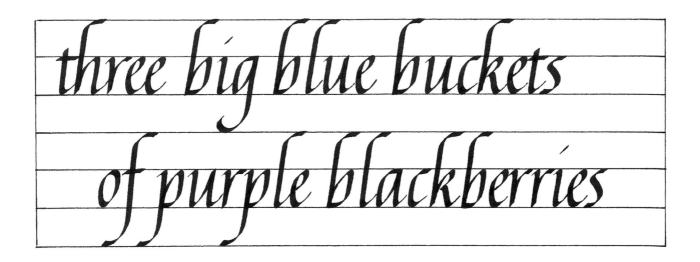

three big blue buckets
of purple blackberries

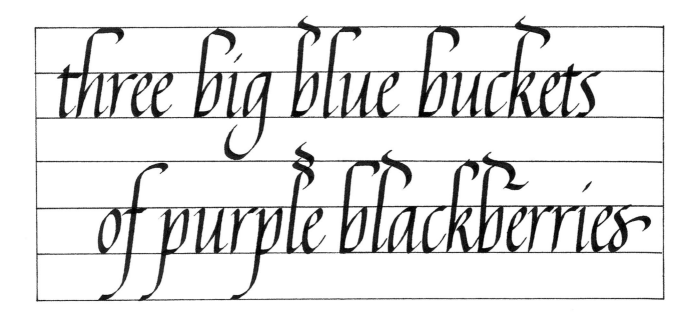

three big blue buckets
of purple blackberries

three big blue buckets
of purple blackberries

8

Simple Italic Capitals

*I*talic capitals can be written in several different ways. They can be simple or decorative. Here's a quick review of **swash capitals,** which are a little more decorative than the simple ones.

SWASH CAPITALS: A Quick Review

In the example below, the letters were written with a fountain pen. The decorative stroke on the top left of many of the letters is called a "swash."

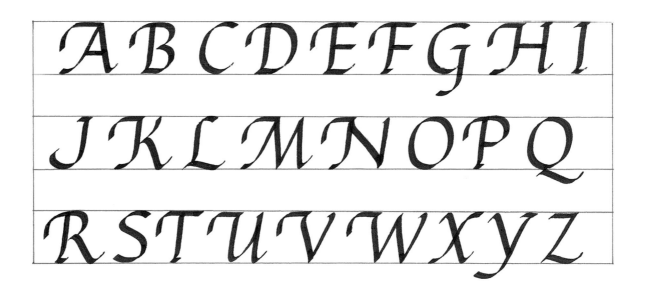

Here are a few points to remember about swash capitals.

1. Swash capitals are slanted, just like Italic minuscules.

2. Their height is about halfway between the height of the smaller minuscules (like the **a, c,** and **e**) and the taller ones (the **h, l,** and **k**).

3. Don't forget to hold your pen in the **diagonal** (45-degree) **pen position,** the same as for the lowercase letters.

SIMPLE CAPITALS

The simple capitals are a whole other story. We call them *simple* because they are less decorative than swash capitals, but that doesn't really mean that they are easier. In fact, you are probably at just the right level to learn them now if you've been practicing your Italic calligraphy for a while.

The simple capitals are written with your pen in the **flattened** (30-degree) **pen position,** which looks like this.

Just to make things a little more complicated, most of the strokes will be made in this pen position, but some other strokes will be made in the diagonal pen position! But that's for a little later....

Basic Facts to Remember About Simple Caps

1. Italic simple capitals are almost the same as Roman capitals, except that **Roman capitals** are vertical, and simple capitals are slanted (the same as Italic lowercase letters and swash capitals). For a quick review of Roman capitals, see Chapter 13, "Writing in Capitals." Also, the simple capitals are a little shorter than the Roman.

2. Simple capitals are also a little shorter than swash capitals. Here's an example of both kinds of capitals, showing their height compared with the height of the minuscules.

3. The simple capitals can be divided into family groups, just like the minuscules. You can begin with some basic strokes and shapes.

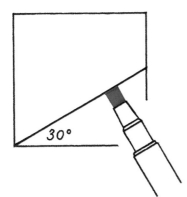

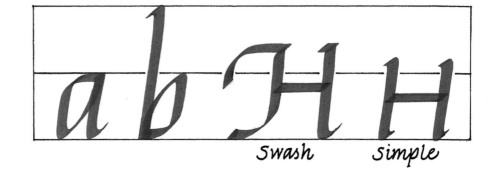

Swash   Simple

Basic Strokes & Shapes

Using a 3.5-mm marker and the standard Italic Guide Lines #1 on page 115, start with some **basic downstrokes.** You can estimate the height of these letters by making them a little taller than the **waistline,** as shown in the illustrations at right. (The waistline is a dotted line.) Be sure that your pen is in the flattened pen position.

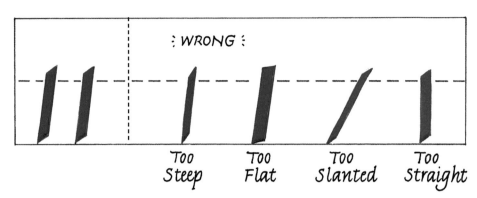

Some of the strokes begin and end with **entrance** and **exit strokes.** These are very small and need to be made slowly.

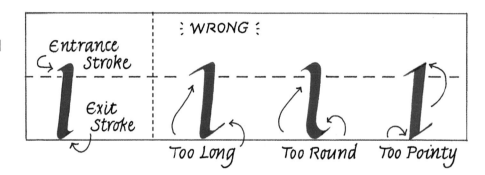

The **O-shape** is another basic form of these capitals. It looks like this.

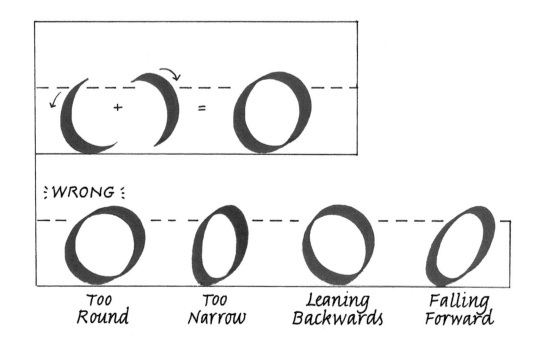

The Letters

Using the basic downstroke, the entrance and exit strokes, and a horizontal line, you can make the
E, F, H, I, L, and **T.**

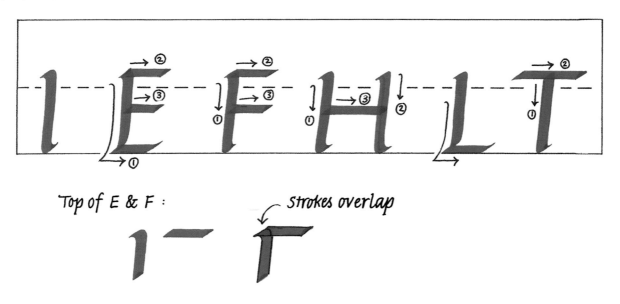

Top of E & F :

Strokes overlap

If you can make the O-shape, you can also make the **C, G,** and **Q.** All of these letters start with
the first stroke of the **O.** The **Q** is an **O** with a "tail." The tops of the **C** and **G** are what's called a
flattened curve.

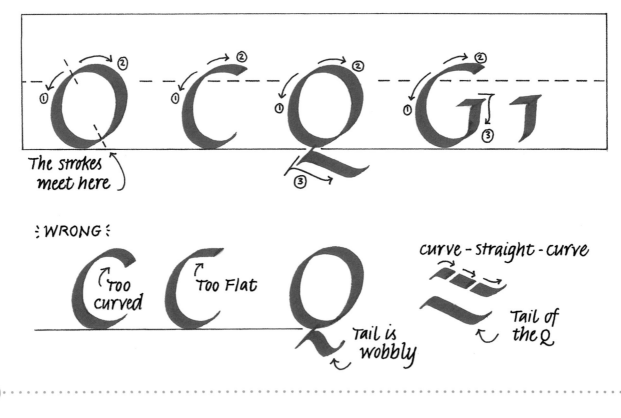

The strokes
meet here

⸭WRONG⸭

Too
curved

Too Flat

Tail is
wobbly

curve - straight - curve

Tail of
the Q

The **B, D, P,** and **R** begin with the basic downstroke, but they have some curved strokes as well. Notice that the bottom of the **B** and **D** are almost the same as the bottom of the **L**. The tops of these letters are made with the same overlapping strokes as the **E** and the **F**.

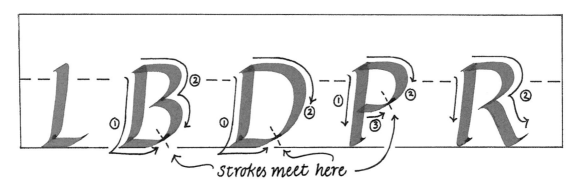

Now try the **S, U,** and **Z.** The **S** has the same kind of flattened curve at the top and the bottom that you make on the **C** and **G.** The curve at the bottom of the **U** is also similar to the **C** and **G.**

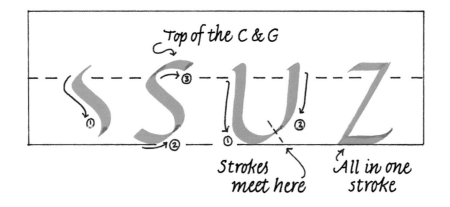

The rest of the simple capitals—**A, M, N, V, W, X,** and **Y**—are all written using two pen positions, the diagonal (45-degree) and the flattened (30-degree). Before you panic, here's a very easy rule to remember.

All the diagonal strokes from upper left to lower right are made with the pen in the diagonal pen position. All other strokes are made in the flattened pen position.

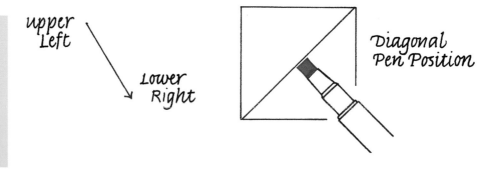

In the illustration below, the strokes made in the diagonal pen position are all in blue and everything else is in violet.

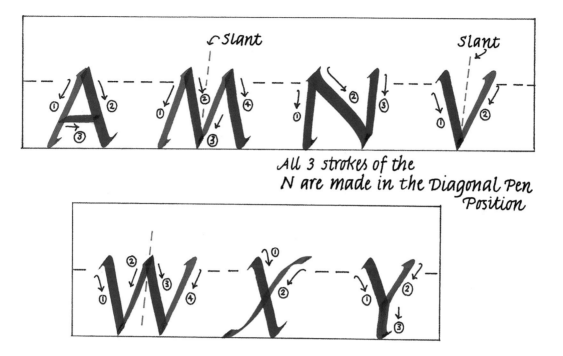

All 3 strokes of the N are made in the Diagonal Pen Position

You'll probably need to spend some extra time practicing these letters, especially the **M** and **W**, where you have to switch from one pen position to the other twice!

If switching pen positions in the middle of a letter is too difficult, you can make all the simple capitals holding the pen in the flattened position (30 degrees). The **A, M, N, V, W, X,** and **Y** will look like the letters below.

They don't look terrible, but they do look nicer if you remember to change your pen position for the diagonal strokes.

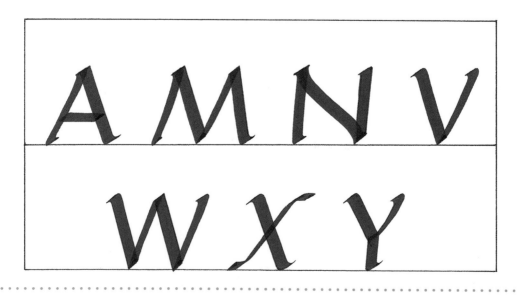

The Whole Alphabet

Here are all the simple capitals in A-B-C form, written with a fountain pen.

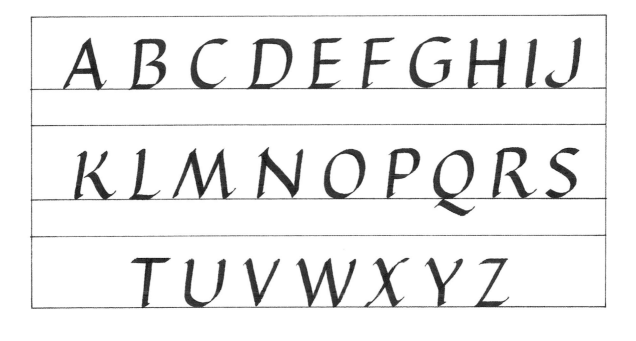

USING SIMPLE CAPITALS WITH MINUSCULES

The simple capitals work very well with Italic minuscules. It's important to remember that the simple capitals are written mostly with the pen in the flattened (30-degree) pen position, and the Italic minuscules are all written in the diagonal (45-degree) pen position. There can be a lot of switching back and forth when you write names or other words that begin with a simple capital. This can be a little tricky until you get used to it.

In the example on page 42, the capitals are underlined so that you'll notice the changing pen positions.

The Pen Position of the Capitals is Different from that of the Lowercase.

You can use simple capitals along with minuscules with shorter, simplified ascenders, or create **contrast** by combining them with the taller, more decorative letters presented in Chapter 5. See which you prefer. If you pick words or names that have ascenders, you'll be able to see the difference pretty clearly.

The names below were written with a fountain pen. The x-height is the standard length (five pen widths), but the ascenders are either shorter or longer than the standard.

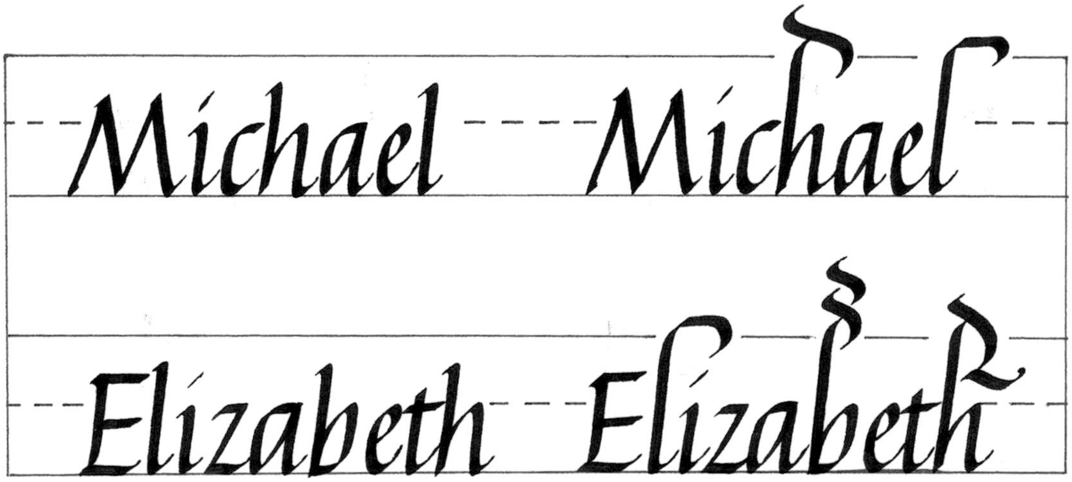

Michael   Michael

Elizabeth   Elizabeth

If you try writing the same name using all the possibilities discussed in the last few pages, you'll see that you can now use Italic in many new ways. All the names below were written with a 2-mm marker.

Emily   Emily   Emily

Emily   Emily

Emily   Emily   Emily

Emily   Emily

9

Italic Handwriting

How many people really like their handwriting? Can it be changed? Well, it may not be easy to repair or relearn handwriting, but one thing you can do is turn your Italic calligraphy into a sort of substitute handwriting.

In this chapter, you'll start with some ordinary writing tools—a #2 pencil and a pointed marker or gel pen. You'll be making **monoline** letters, that is, letters with a single thickness. Then you'll switch to fountain pens to get the full effect of the thick and thin strokes of Italic letters.

Begin with the skeleton forms of the letters, shortening the length of the ascenders and descenders as you did in Chapter 5.

Use any paper with lines and try these letters using either a pencil or a pointed marker. You can also try this with a gel pen, which is very soft and nice to write with.

a b c d e f g h i j k l m n
o p q r s t u v w x y z

What makes this a handwriting?

Speed—Well, not exactly *speed*, but you do write a little more quickly.

Connections—When you make words, some of the letters can be connected to each other without taking the pen off the paper. Some of the other letters can also be connected, but the pen will need to be lifted and moved. You'll see how this works in just a moment.

Look at the difference between the writing in the words below.

underneath   minimal

underneath   minimal

The first line was written in what's called **formal Italic.** The letters are carefully spaced, and each letter is made separately.

The two words on the second line were written in **Italic handwriting.** All the letters are touching, and some are made slightly differently from the standard way of writing Italic letters.

A few little variations in the letters can be used to make the letters join or connect with one another. In the examples that follow, the letters were made with a gel pen. Later we'll switch to fountain pens or calligraphy markers.

In the skeleton alphabet at the beginning of this chapter, the tops of the **b, h, k,** and **l** have no entrance strokes. If you leave out the little curve or hook at the top, you can join other letters to them without stopping.

ab ih ak ul

You can also connect letters that end with an exit stroke (the **a, c, d, h, i, k, l, m, n, t** and **u**) to the other letters that start with entrance strokes (the **i, j, m, n, p, r, u,** and **y**) in the same way, by leaving out the first little curve, like this.

i becomes *i*   *n* becomes *n*

b becomes *b*   *p* becomes *p*

So here's the rule

Any letter that ends with an exit stroke can connect to a letter that begins with an entrance stroke by leaving out the entrance stroke on the second letter.

ai aj am an ap ar au ay

If the word you are writing starts with a letter that has an entrance stroke, you don't need to take it out.

mum looks better than *mum*

You can connect the **o** to the next letter by adding a little curve at the end of the **o**. You can connect the **e** to the next letter from the center of the **e**, like this.

ot oh book

en et keep

Notice that there's no connection between the **b** and the **o** in "book." Some letters can't connect; they are the **b**, **g**, **j**, **p**, **q**, and **y**.

Be extra careful with your spacing when you use these letters in words.

ba go je pa yo

But if the letter following the **b**, **g**, **j**, **p**, **q**, or **y** starts with an entrance stroke, you can attach that letter to the one before it. You'll need to lift your pen, but the letters will still be connected. Make the entrance stroke of the second letter a little longer than usual, so that the letters won't be too close together.

b + r = br   p + u = pu

WRONG: *br pu*

Too close

There are other times when you need to stop and lift (or move) your pen between letters, even though the letters will appear to be connected. With these **a-shape** letters—**a**, **c**, **d**, **g**, and **q**—if the letter before it has an exit stroke, it will look as if you wrote without stopping. But in fact you will need to move your pen before starting the a-shape.

n + a = na   i + g = ig

stop here and
move the pen to
the top of the a.

stop here
and move pen to
the top of the g.

There are also a few letter variations you can try. This is what they look like.

s   kiss   test   *Try this too!*

Stop here) and move the pen before starting 2nd s.

v w   lawn have

Start v & w like this if a letter connects to them)

You can connect the **v** and **w** to the next letter with the same kind of curve you make at the end of the **o.** You can also curve the ending of the **r** a little to connect it to the letter that follows.

vi wo ru hurry

Always remember to watch your spacing! The space between letters is very important. Here again is the spacing rule.

The space between letters should appear to be about the same as the space inside the letters.

Write a short piece using a pencil, a pointed marker, a gel pen, or even a ballpoint pen. Try to connect the letters whenever you can, keeping in mind that sometimes you'll be able to do it without lifting your pen, and other times you'll need to lift it. Use your simple capitals with Italic handwriting. They look good written monoline (without thick or thin lines).

Now try using your fountain pen for some Italic handwriting practice. Write a few names, like this.

Barbara Michael

Dolores Florence

Margaret Samuel

Italic handwriting, whether written with a fountain pen or any other pen or marker, can be used for writing a letter to a friend, making a birthday card or valentine, or even making some casual stationery for yourself. In Chapter 16, you'll learn how to do that.

10

Swing Gothic

Gothic calligraphy comes from the Middle Ages, before the invention of the printing press. At that time, more than 700 years ago, all books were written by hand. The style of calligraphy used in many of these books consisted of tall, narrow letters written very close together. Sometimes the term **Black Letter** is used in place of **Gothic** to describe this calligraphy.

Gothic can be very lively and decorative. In fact, it's what many people think of when they hear the word *calligraphy.*

There were many different ways that the scribes of the Middle Ages made their Gothic letters. You may be familiar with the Gothic alphabet known as **Textura.** We're going to take a look at this alphabet and then do it a different way, changing the letters—which tend to be rather stiff and narrow—to give them a little more bounce. But first, let's look at Textura.

A QUICK REVIEW OF TEXTURA

The basic lowercase letters of Textura Gothic are made up of very simple strokes, most of which are either vertical or diagonal. The pen position is diagonal (45 degrees). To practice or review these letters using your 3.5-mm markers, use Guide Lines #9 on page 122. Here are three basic letters, the **i, n,** and **o.**

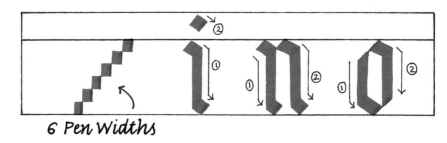

6 Pen Widths

In fact, if you know how to make these three letters, you can pretty much do the whole alphabet.

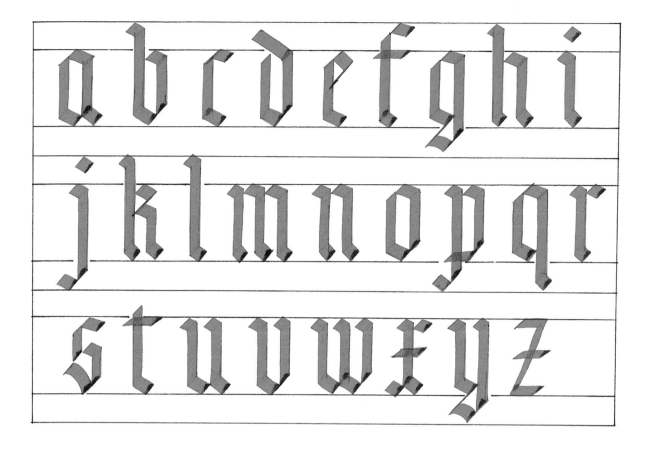

Spacing

One of the most important things to remember about Gothic is that the white space between the strokes is very narrow, just slightly wider than the strokes themselves. And the space between letters is about equal to the white space inside the letters.

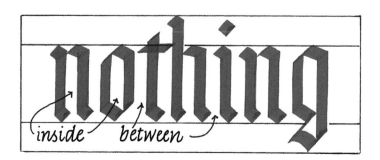

Swing Gothic

Swing Gothic is my own name for a lively, looser version of the basic Textura. This alphabet is made in the same (diagonal) pen position as Textura, using the same guide lines. Although the downstrokes in this style remain straight and tall, you add some extra movement to the tops and bottoms of some of the strokes. Move your pen slowly, or the slight curves at the tops and bottoms of the strokes may become exaggerated.

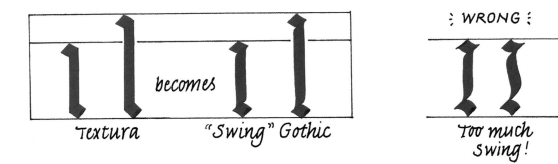

Here is the Swing Gothic alphabet.

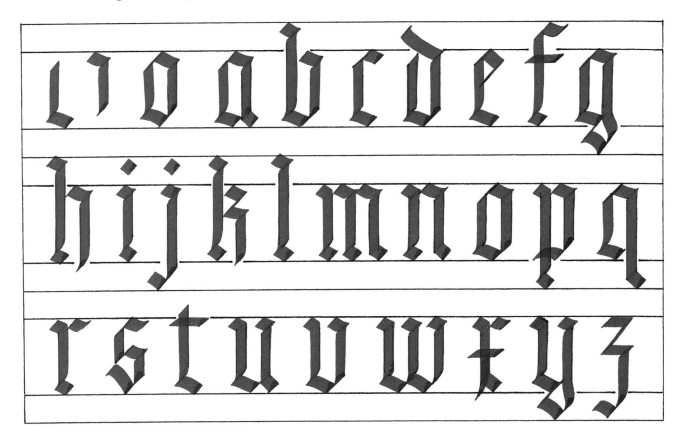

In this alphabet, the swing is put in sometimes and left out at other times. The *beginning* of the **m, n, p, r, u, v, w, x,** and **y** is made with a simple (non-curving) stroke, as is the *ending* of the **a, m, n, q, u,** and **x.**

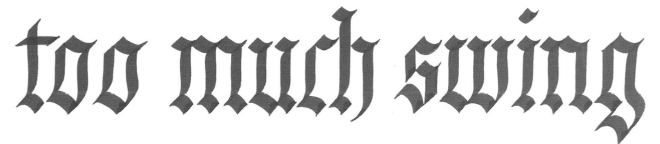

If there's too much swing in your Swing Gothic, the letters get too wiggly.

Try writing a few words or a short quotation using this alphabet. Even though the letters are very similar to Textura Gothic, a line of writing looks much livelier when you loosen up a little. This example was done with a fountain pen. The first two lines are in Textura and the next two are in Swing Gothic. Use Guide Lines #10 on page 122 for Textura and Swing Gothic, with a B or B-3 fountain pen or 2-mm marker.

11

Modern Gothic
An Alphabet with Many Names

*J*umping way ahead to the twentieth century, we come to a modern Gothic style that is easy to read and the most fun to write. This alphabet is sometimes called **Gothicized Italic** because of the way the letters begin and end with thin lines and seem to dance along on the page as they do in Italic.

A very famous English calligrapher named Edward Johnston invented this alphabet. He used it in his artwork and sometimes referred to it as **Black Italic.** Here's an example of his writing.

The letters presented here are a little different from the ones that Edward Johnston made, but we'll try to keep the Johnston flair in this version of his calligraphy. Because this alphabet came along 700 years after Textura Gothic, we'll call it **Modern Gothic.**

The pen position for this alphabet is the same as for Italic: the diagonal position, or 45-degree pen angle. The ascenders and descenders are shorter than the x-height. Use Guide Lines #11 on page 123. The proportions are the same as those of Italic minuscule variations, but these letters are vertical and Italic is slanted.

Here are some basic strokes. Notice the difference between the basic downstrokes of Textura and Modern Gothic. Instead of a sharp angle between the vertical line and the diagonal line as in Textura, Modern Gothic has a curve or bend.

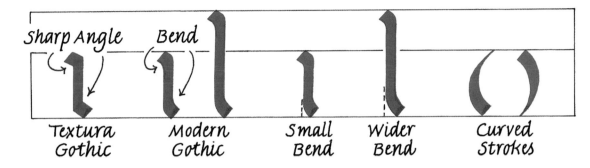

Try beginning and ending the basic downstroke with a thin line, similar to the entrance and exit strokes in Italic.

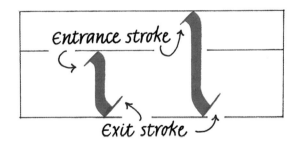

Now try making a few downstrokes that connect to each other by means of their entrance strokes. Start each stroke inside the previous stroke, like this.

Notice that the white space between the strokes is narrow. It's a little wider than the strokes themselves. Also, the white space has a very special shape, like the shape of a Gothic church window or a Gothic arch. This is what it looks like.

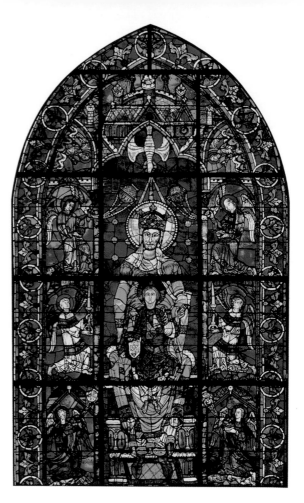

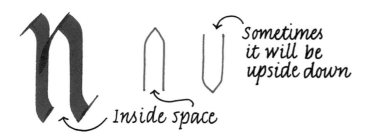

sometimes it will be upside down

Inside space

Like most other alphabets, many of the letters of Modern Gothic are built on these few simple strokes and shapes. Be sure to notice that almost all the Modern Gothic letters have sharp points at the top or the bottom, or both.

Using the **basic downstroke,** we can make the **m, n, h, r,** and **u.**

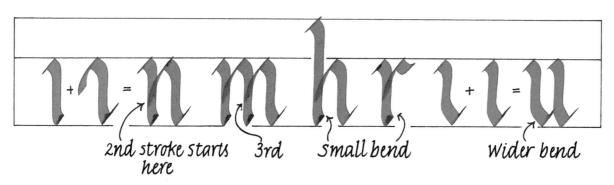

2nd stroke starts here   *3rd*   *small bend*   *wider bend*

The **straight-line family** of letters consists of the i, j, t, l, and f. On some of these, the bend at the bottom is bigger (wider) and on others, it's smaller (narrower).

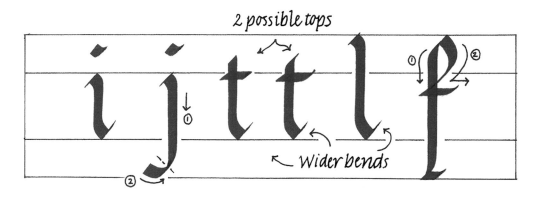

With the two **curved strokes** and a few extra little strokes, we can make the o, c, e, a, q, d, and x.

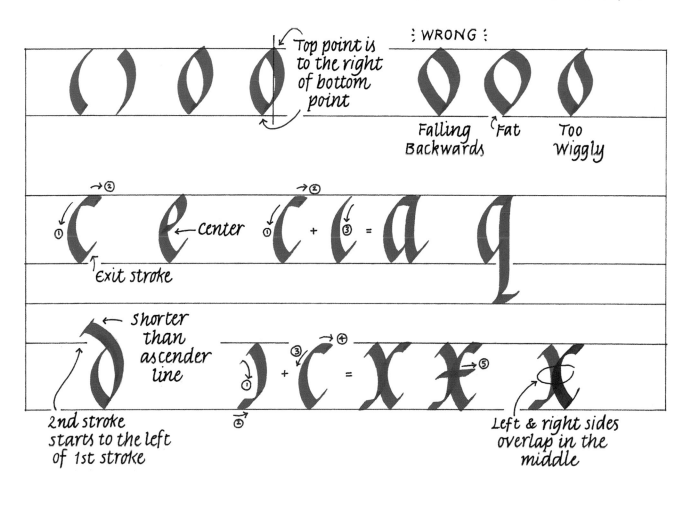

You can combine the downstroke and the curve to make the **b, v,** and **w.**

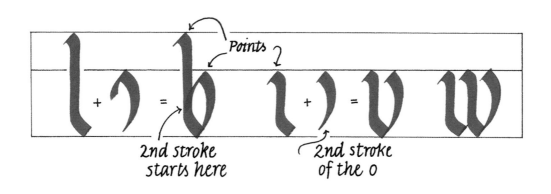

The **s** and **z** are a little different. Be sure that they are narrow and pointy so they fit with the other Modern Gothic letters.

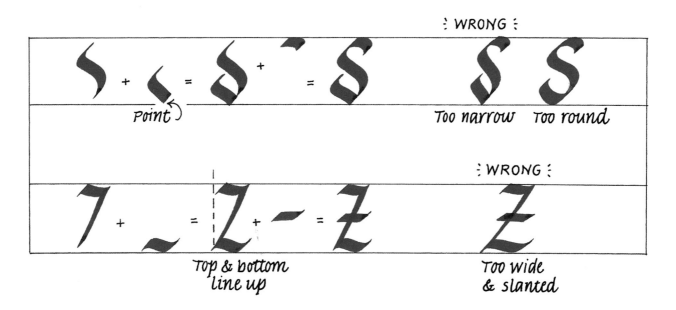

Here are some letters that are similar, but with a few special strokes—the **p**, **g**, **y**, and **k**.

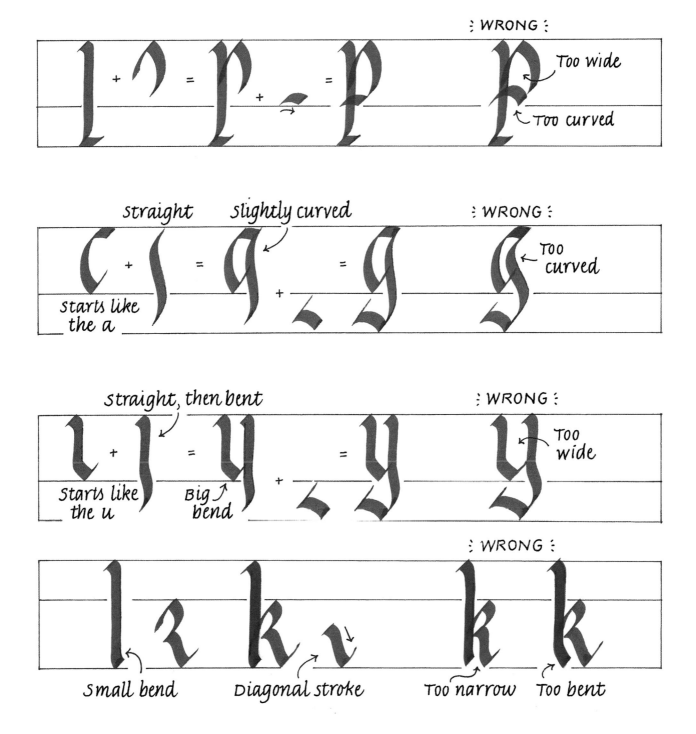

: WRONG :

Too wide

Too curved

straight   slightly curved

: WRONG :

Too curved

starts like the a

straight, then bent

: WRONG :

Too wide

Starts like the u   Big bend

: WRONG :

Small bend   Diagonal stroke   Too narrow   Too bent

Spacing

When writing words with these letters, try to keep the white spaces *visually equal,* meaning that the white space *inside* the letters and the space *between* the letters should be about the same.

But what makes writing this alphabet special is that the thin exit strokes—and sometimes the entrance strokes—will often make the letters connect to each other, sort of like Italic or Italic handwriting. Here's an example.

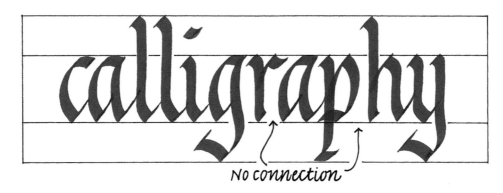

No connection

Of course, some letters can't connect with each other, such as **be, oe, gl, sa,** and other letter combinations that don't have entrance or exit strokes. Try to allow the correct amount of white space between them so they look as if they belong to each other, even if they don't touch.

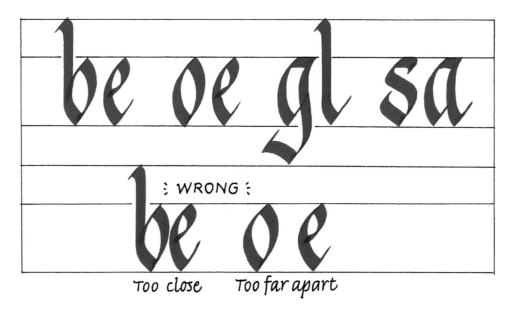

WRONG

Too close   Too far apart

Write a couple of sentences or a short poem in Modern Gothic. See how many connections you can make between letters. Also look at the shapes of the white spaces inside and between the letters. This is called the **negative space,** and it is a very important part of learning calligraphy.

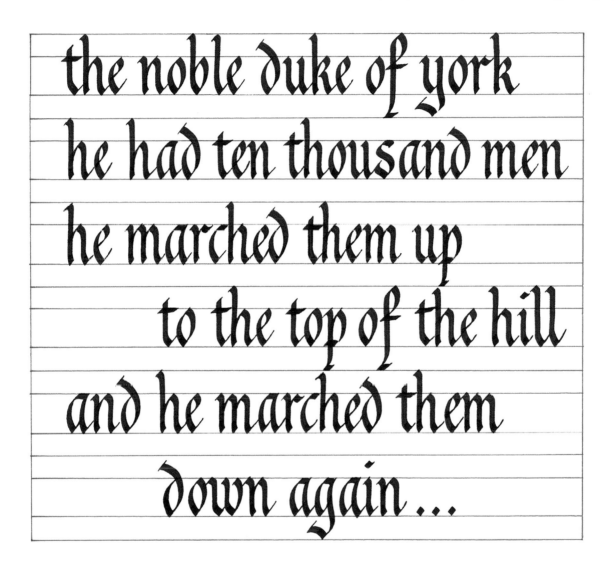

Something Extra

One other way Modern Gothic can look more Gothic (as opposed to looking more Italic) is by making a pointy top or **serif** on certain letters. We call this top a **beak serif** because it looks a little like a bird's beak.

This stroke is made in two separate parts, like this.

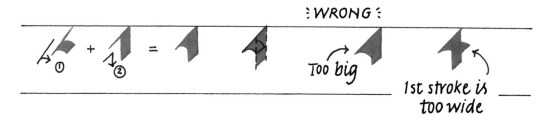

You can start the **b, h, i, j, k, l,** and **p** with the serif, and you can also put it on the right side of the **u** and the **y.**

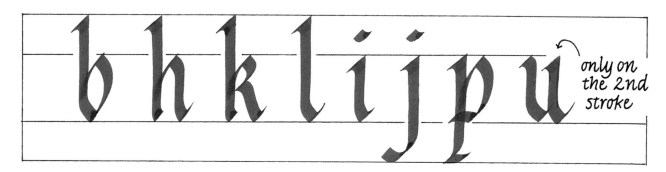

Letter Variations

Modern Gothic is especially fun to learn because there are so many letter variations. Here are some extra lowercase letters that you can try. Be sure to notice that the ascenders and descenders are sometimes longer and sometimes shorter than the standard Modern Gothic letters. Remember that any variation shown for the top of the **b** can also be used on the **h, k,** and **l.**

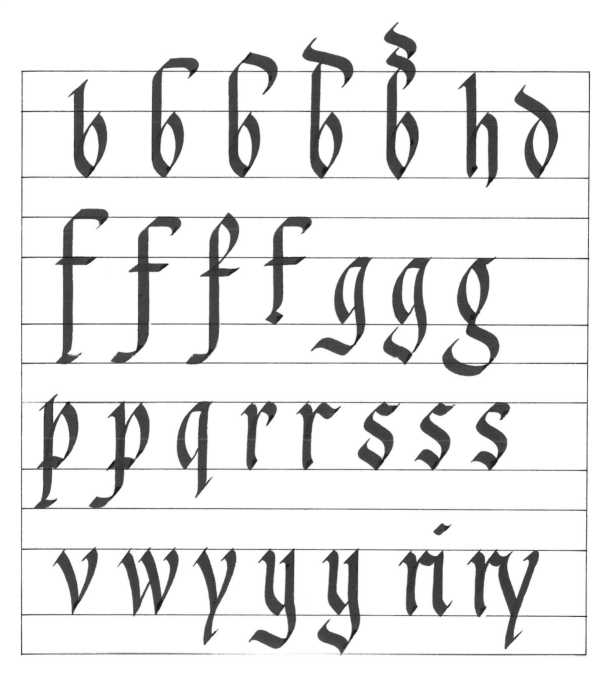

As a good exercise, pick a word with ascenders and/or descenders and try to write it as many ways as you can, using all the letter variations. Here's an example. This was done with a fountain pen, using Guide Lines #12.

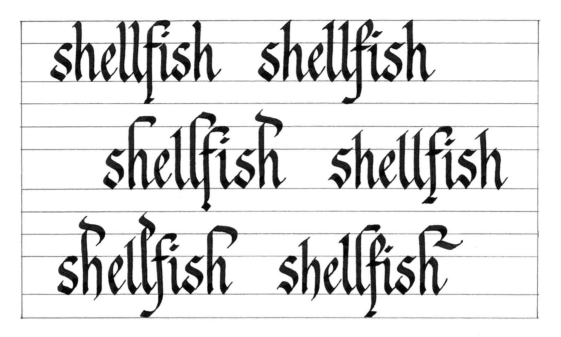

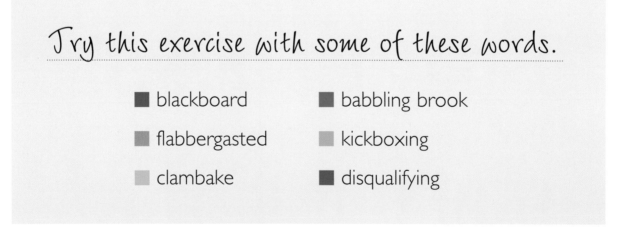

Try this exercise with some of these words.

- ■ blackboard
- ■ flabbergasted
- ■ clambake
- ■ babbling brook
- ■ kickboxing
- ■ disqualifying

12

Modern Gothic Capitals

A whole book could be written about Gothic capitals. In the Middle Ages, when books were copied (by hand, you'll remember!), it was usually the job of one or more scribes to write the minuscule letters and of another calligrapher to make the capital letters.

Depending on the importance of the sentence or the part of the book, the capitals could be big or small, more or less colorful, very simple or very decorative, or anything in between. The more important the word (or paragraph or chapter), the bigger and more ornamental the capital letter would be.

From one book to another, even from one *part* of a book to another, there was so much variety in the shape and form of Gothic capitals that it is impossible to pick one alphabet of Gothic capitals and say that it is the one you should learn or use. The best you can do is to find capitals that look right with the style of Gothic minuscules you're using.

As a general rule, though, whatever capitals you use with your Gothic minuscules, they should always be in *contrast* to the lowercase. Usually they are wider and more open-looking than the narrow minuscules.

In addition to serving as a contrast to the minuscules, Gothic capitals must also have some shapes or strokes in common with the lowercase letters.

Modern Gothic minuscules are somewhat free and bouncy. Choosing a capital alphabet that has some strokes that "match" the lowercase letters and that feels sort of casual is always a good idea.

Pen Position, Height and Basic Strokes

For these capital letters, keep your pen in the same position as the minuscules: the diagonal or 45-degree pen position. The height of these capitals is about halfway between the x-height (height of the smaller lowercase letters, like the **a, c, e,** and **x**) and the height of the letters with ascenders. This is the same rule as for making Italic capitals. Here are some basic strokes.

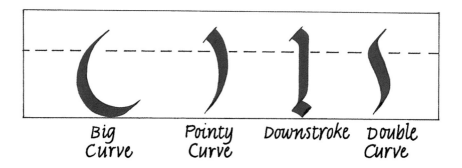

Big Curve   Pointy Curve   Downstroke   Double Curve

Using the basic strokes, we can divide the letters into groups.

Big Curve Letters: C, E, G, O, Q, T

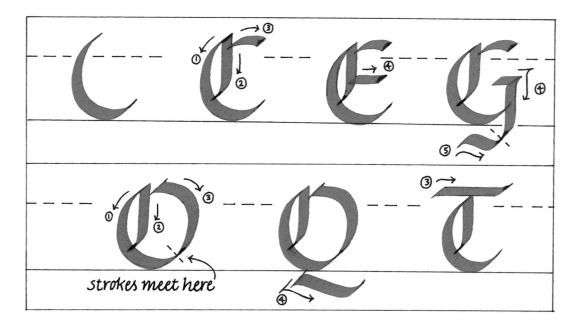

strokes meet here

These letters are round and the same as, or similar to, Textura Gothic capitals.

Pointy Curve Letters: B, D, P, R

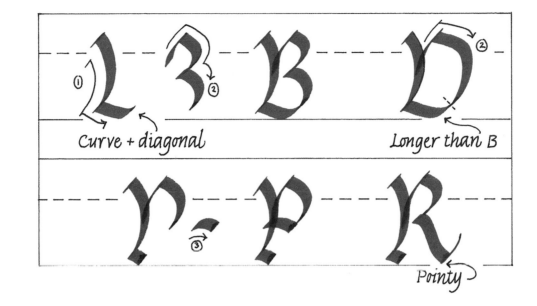

Double Curve Letters: J, L, U, V, W, Y

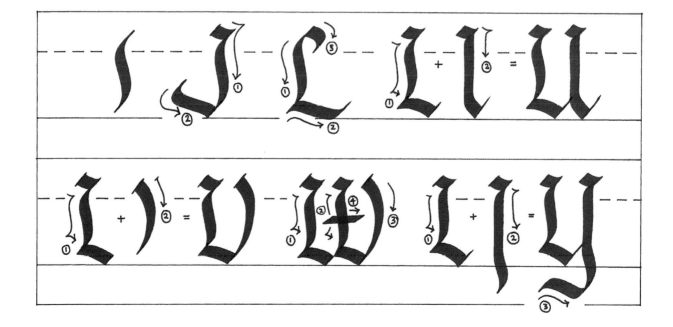

Downstroke Letters: F, H, I, K, N

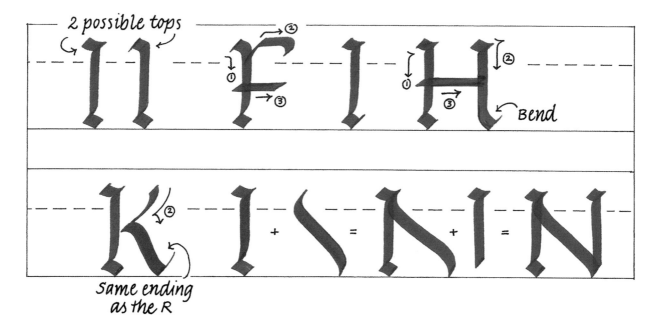

Exceptions: A, M, S, X, Z

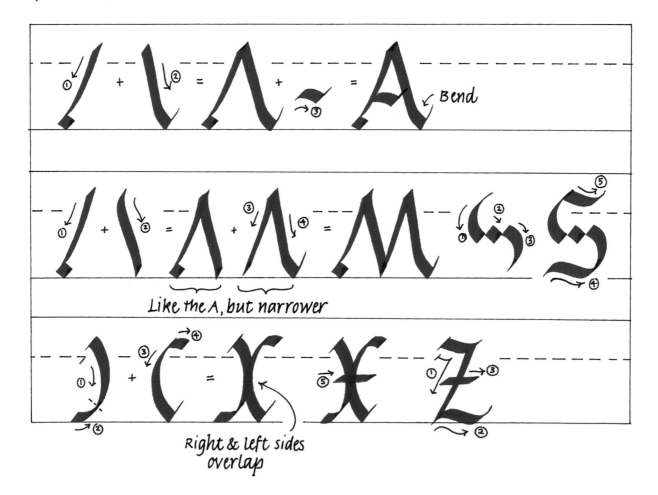

Write some names or words starting with these capitals and using the Modern Gothic minuscules. Try including some of the minuscule variations, such as these.

Daniel Jeanette Laurie

Margaret Thomas Kathryn

Heather Roberta etc.

Hint You can change
the effect of Modern Gothic lowercase letters
by using other styles of capitals with them, such as double-
stroke Gothic capitals or Roman capitals. Look for more
examples of these letters in other
calligraphy books.

Angela Angela Angela

Diane Diane Diane

13

Writing in Capitals

From time to time, you'll get a chance to write something in all capitals. When do you use all capitals? Write in capitals FOR EMPHASIS, to make something seem IMPORTANT, to get someone's ATTENTION...or just because you feel like it.

It's important to know which kinds of letters to use when writing in capitals. It's also very important to spend some extra time practicing spacing.

In Chapter 8, you learned the simple Italic capitals. These letters are loosely based on Roman capitals, which you may already have learned.

A QUICK REVIEW OF ROMAN CAPITALS

These were made with a wide fountain pen (B-3 or B). They are a little taller than simple capitals. Simple capitals slant, like the Italic minuscules. Roman capitals are vertical. You can try these letters using the same guide lines you use for Modern Gothic, estimating the height (taller than the waistline, shorter than the ascender line).

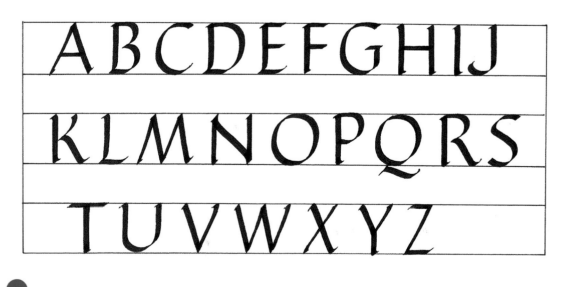

As you can see, Roman capitals are a vertical version of the simple Italic capitals. When you practice either alphabet, it's a good idea to *write slowly* and practice the letters in groups, according to their basic shapes.

If you'd like to write words in capitals, use either the simple Italic capitals or the Roman capitals. Simple (*undecorated*) letters are far easier to read than more ornamental ones, such as Italic swash capitals or Gothic capitals.

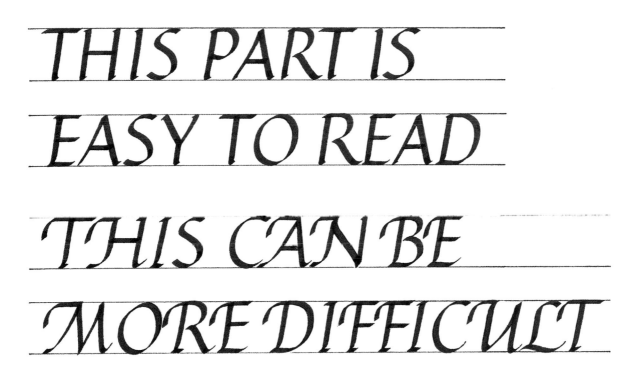

THIS PART IS
EASY TO READ
THIS CAN BE
MORE DIFFICULT

Practice your spacing by coloring in the space between letters with a colored pencil, like this.

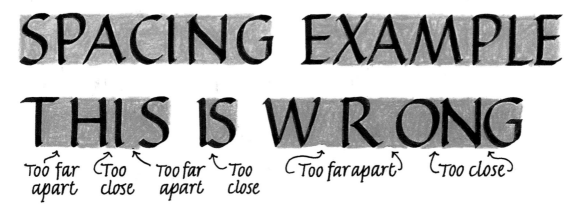

SPACING EXAMPLE
THIS IS WRONG

Too far apart   Too close   Too far apart   Too close   Too far apart   Too close

When writing in capitals, you can try putting the written lines close together. Because these capital letters have relatively simple shapes, they are easy to read even when the writing lines are near each other. As an experiment, try writing the same text with the lines far apart and then close together.

This would definitely not be legible if you did the same thing using Gothic capitals!

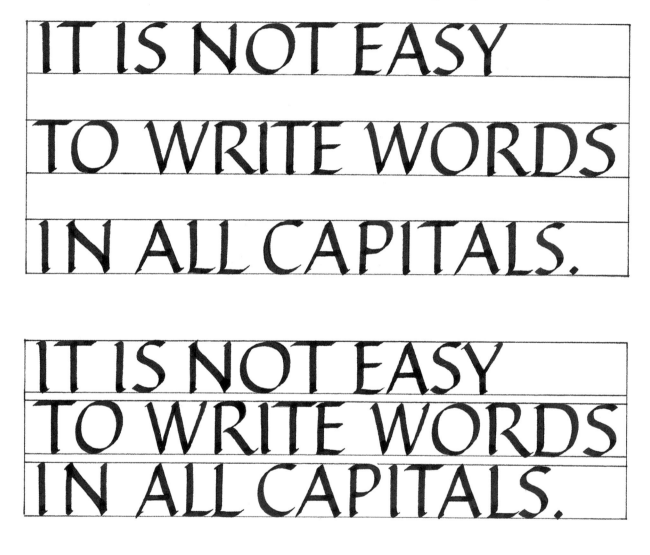

In Chapter 18, "Making Signs," you'll have an opportunity to write in all capitals. A sign is a good example of where writing your message in capital letters can really help make your point.

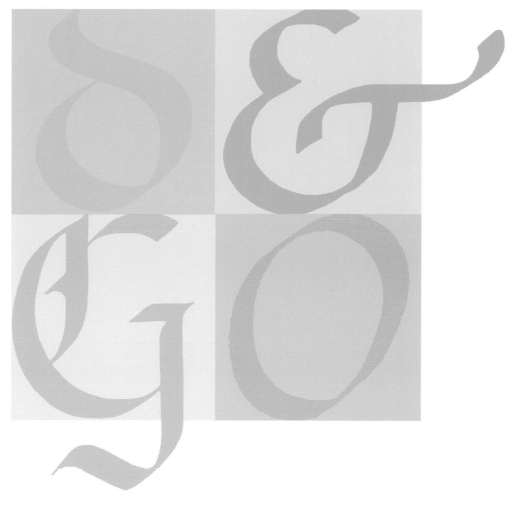

PART III

Creative PROJECTS

14

Writing Larger

Although there are lots of mechanical ways to "blow up" (increase the size of) your calligraphy—by using a copy machine or a computer—it's also fun to make larger letters by hand with your pens or markers.

In order to make signs and posters, or to write a LARGE message, or perhaps to write large initials on your personal stationery, you'll need to write with wider nibs.

Whatever size marker you choose to write with, it's important to remember that the height of the letter is in proportion to the width of the pen (sorry...more math). For Italic, the x-height is five times the width of the nib (see Chapter 6). If you use your 3.5-mm marker, the x-height space looks like this.

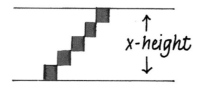

If the nib (or marker) is narrower, the space to write in will be shorter. If the nib is wider, the space will be taller.

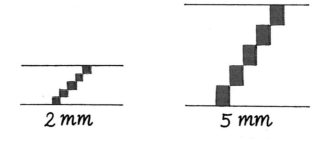

2 mm   5 mm

Calligraphy markers with a 5-mm width are usually fairly easy to find in art supply or stationery stores. Sometimes you'll find markers with two ends, one measuring 5 mm and the other 2 mm. Let's compare the 5-mm to the 3.5-mm marker that you've been using.

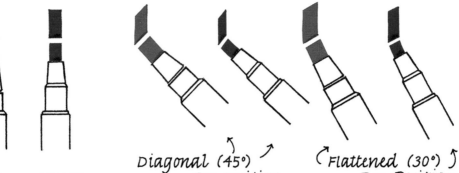

5 mm   3.5 mm

Diagonal (45°) Pen Position   Flattened (30°) Pen Position

Since the x-height for Italic minuscules is five times the width of the nib, the x-height for the 5-mm nib will be 5 × 5 mm, or 25 millimeters (which is the same as 2.5 centimeters). It will look like this.

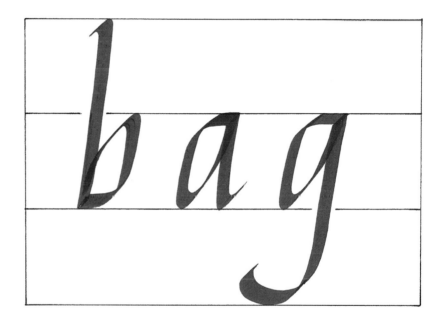

Using Guide Lines #13 on page 124, try writing Italic with a 5-mm marker. Remember that the simple capital letters will be taller than the x-height and shorter than the ascender, like this.

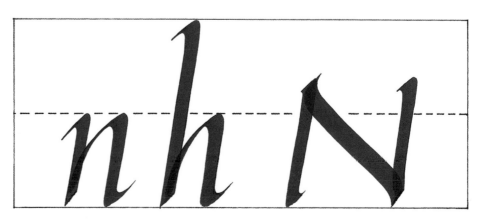

As you can see, you'll need larger paper if you want to write more than a word or two! In fact, the space between the lines in this example has been reduced to make it fit on one page.

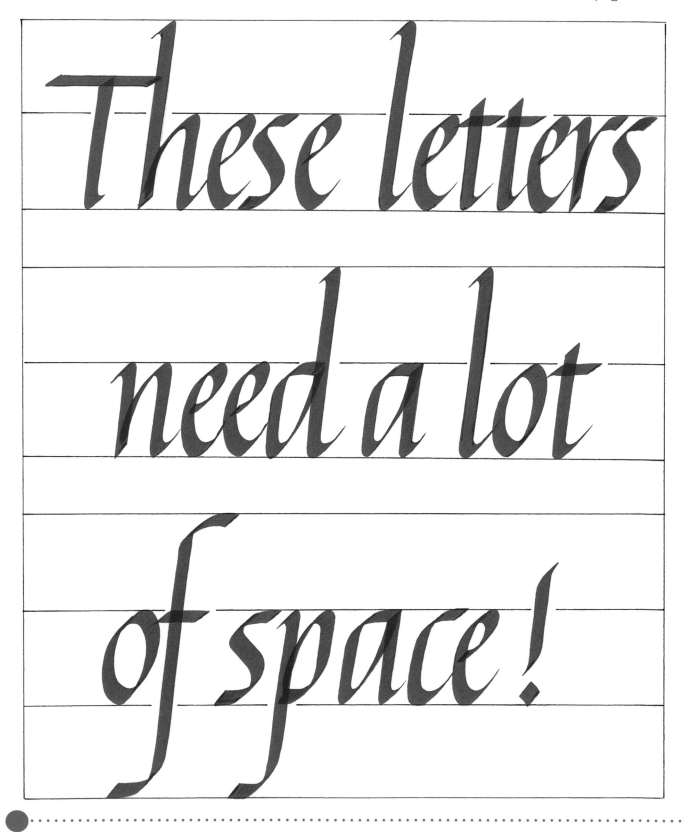

You might like to try designing some personal stationery using your 5-mm marker (see Chapter 16). A name (or initials) written with a 5-mm marker gives a very different message from one written with a smaller nib. A name written with a small nib says, "How do you do?"

One written larger says, "HERE I AM!"

In the back of this book you'll find guide lines for Textura or Swing Gothic (#14) and Modern Gothic (#15) to use with a 5-mm marker (see pages 125 and 126). You can also try other styles of calligraphy with your 5-mm pen.

Hint Try standing up when writing larger. Your arm movements will be freer, so the longer strokes will be easier to make than when you are sitting down with your arm resting on the table. Large writing is more *arm* movement than *hand* movement.

DOUBLE PENCILS

Here's another way to work large. Take two pencils and use either tape or a rubber band to hold them together, being sure that the points line up.

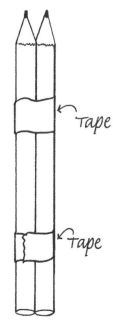

Tape

Tape

You can write (or draw) any alphabet using this double-pencil tool. Hold the tool so the points form a "pen angle," either diagonal or flattened, just like a marker or fountain pen.

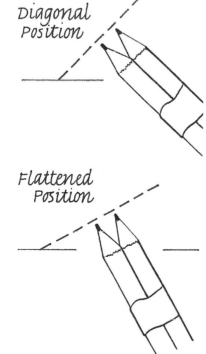

Diagonal Position

Flattened Position

You'll need to draw some lines (or find some lined paper) that will give you the correct letter height. Then try writing with your double pencils, like this.

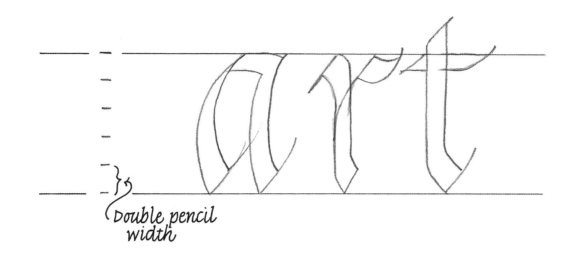

Double pencil width

Hint If you outline the letters with a marker and then fill them in with a different color marker or paint, it's a good idea to make the outline using a *waterproof* marker. That way the outline won't "bleed into" (mix with) the second color.

You'll see that when you write with double pencils, sometimes the tops or bottoms of the letters are open. Just add a line with one of the pencils to close the letters. It's very easy.

After you make your letters with double pencils, you can finish them in a variety of ways.

You can use pointed markers to outline them and then fill in the letters using different color markers, colored pencils, or paint.

You can even decorate the insides of the letters with patterns, stripes, dots, or multi-colored designs.

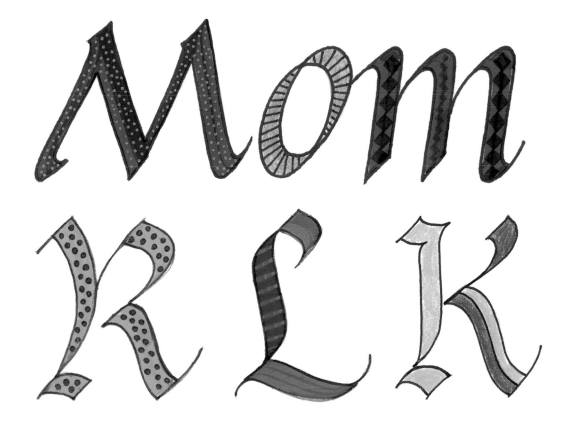

Hint   You can use your double pencils to draw the letters on other surfaces besides paper—such as wood or heavy cardboard (for making signs)—and then fill in the pencil outlines using paint or markers. You'll need to experiment (or ask someone) to find out which paints or markers work on different surfaces.

15

Quotation or Poem

When your friends and family see that you are learning calligraphy, they may ask you to write a favorite quotation or poem for them. Or you may have something of your own that you want to hang on your wall. Here's how to go about figuring out a **layout**.

HOW TO START

When writing a text (a quotation or poem of any length) in calligraphy, there are many decisions to make. Here are some questions to think about.

1. What alphabet should I use?
2. Which pen do I prefer (calligraphy marker or fountain pen)?
3. Do I want to write large, small, or both?
4. Do I want to use one color? Two colors? Black ink (fountain pen)? Black ink and colored marker?

After you have made some of these decisions, it is time to figure out the arrangement of the words or the lines of writing on the page. This is called the layout. It's a good idea to begin by making a few sketches using a pencil or pointed marker. You can hold your paper either vertically or horizontally.

Take a look first at what is called a **flush left** layout, which means all the lines of writing line up under each other and start in the same position at the left-hand margin.

This is an example of a layout in which all of the lines of writing begin under each other on the left side of the page. This is called "Flush Left."

This is also a Flush Left layout. In this example the paper is held in the horizontal position, rather than the vertical position.

Other possibilities for layout besides flush left include **flush right, centered,** or **irregular** (sometimes called *rag* or *ragged*) layouts. The examples below show **vertical** layouts, but your layouts can also be **horizontal,** or even **square.**

Flush Right

Centered

Irregular

To help you decide which layout is best, you can write your lines of text with different tools—large and small markers or fountain pens—to see what you prefer. Then cut out the lines in strips with a pair of scissors. Place the strips of paper on a white sheet of paper so that you have a clean background for your calligraphy. (They will be easier to see that way than if you put them directly on the table.) You can move them around to see how they look—to the left, the right, centered, up, and down. Remember to try both vertical and horizontal layouts.

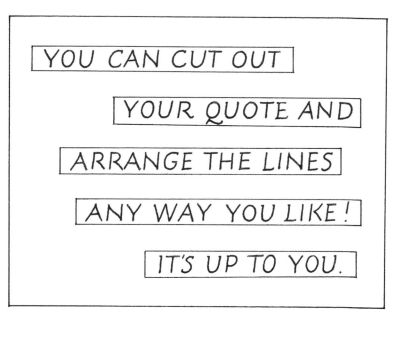

Always leave plenty of extra space around the edges of the writing.

In this example there is white space all around the calligraphy. It looks good and is easy to read.

This page has hardly any white space to the left or the right or the top or the bottom of the calligraphy. It is much too crowded, isn't it? Be sure to leave white space around the text.

Contrast

To make the layout more interesting, you can add some **contrast** to the page. Here's how to do this.

1. Choose a part of the quotation or poem that you think should stand out on the page.

Here are some possibilities.
- the first letter of the text
- the first word
- the first line
- the first letter of each line or each sentence
- some important word or words in the middle

2. You can make this letter, word, or words stand out by writing it bigger, in a different color, or in a different style of calligraphy. Here are some examples.

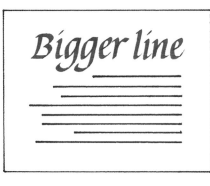

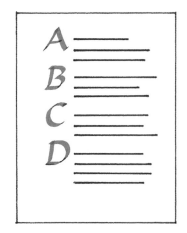

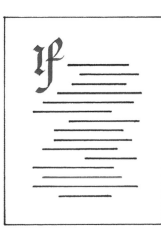

A Few Hot Tips for Layout

1. Leave more space around your quotation than you think you need. You can always cut the paper later to make it smaller, but you can't make it larger if you don't leave enough space.

2. If you want your layout to be centered, try this: Write each line, cut it out, and fold it in half. Draw a light pencil line down the center of your layout paper and match the folded center of each line with the pencil line. Tape the strips of paper in place to see how they look.

3. Tape your lines of writing with removable tape. That way you can keep moving them around until you are satisfied, without tearing the paper.

4. Use your scissors and tape to try different possibilities, such as these.

- substituting a capital letter in a different size, color, or alphabet for the first letter of the quotation
- writing the first line or word in a different size or color
- adding a drawing or border design

What About the Title?

If your quotation or poem has a title and/or author, you may want to include this in your design. Try writing the name of the poem, the title of the book, or the author's name a few different ways and cutting it out. Put the different pieces on your layout page in different places to see where they look good. Here are some possibilities.

- ◾ top, centered
- ◾ top, left or right
- ◾ bottom, centered
- ◾ bottom, left or right

Here are some more ideas.

- ◾ Write the title a little bigger than the text or in a different color.
- ◾ Write the title in capital letters (simple capitals, not decorative) and the poem or quotation in lowercase letters.

- ◾ If the quotation or poem is part of a longer text, such as a line from a book or a poem, you can put the name of the book or poem at the bottom. Start with the word *from*, for example, "from the Bible."

The Finished Piece

When you are satisfied with your layout, you can try doing the calligraphy on a piece of "good" paper. Measure the top and left margins of the layout to see where the writing should begin. Make the same measurements on your "good" paper so that the calligraphy will start in the same place. If your paper isn't too thick, you can place your guide lines under it. If you can't see through it, you'll have to draw lines on the paper. Do this carefully and check it twice before starting the calligraphy.

And don't forget: EVERYONE MAKES MISTAKES! You'll probably need to write your quotation a couple times (at least!) before you are happy with the results.

A good rule

If the title is at the top, make it stand out by writing it either bigger or in capitals. If it is at the bottom, make it smaller, or somehow less important than the text. For example, if you write the quotation in Gothic with a 3.5-mm pen, make the name at the bottom in Italic with a 2-mm pen.

16

Stationery

*E*very calligrapher wants to have his or her own personal stationery. You can, of course, do the calligraphy individually on each sheet of paper, but it probably makes more sense to design it once and have it printed.

Printing can be done in a copy shop or by a "real" printer, but that's putting the cart before the horse. Before you are ready to have your stationery printed, you need to do the calligraphy.

Start by considering two possible paper sizes: unfolded sheets of paper measuring 8½ inches × 11 inches (or A4), which is standard copy-machine size, or folded cards that are made with half sheets of the same size paper. (A4 and 8½ × 11 inches are not exactly the same size but they are close. Copy machines in the U.S. use paper 8½ × 11 inches, and in Europe they use A4.)

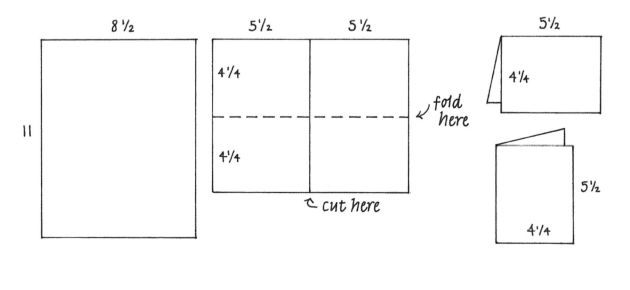

If you use the full-size unfolded sheet, you can make what is called a letterhead—stationery used for writing a letter. The folded card can be used for a shorter letter, a note, a thank-you card, or whatever you'd put on a note card (for example, an invitation).

It's up to you what words to put on your stationery. If you choose the larger-size paper (8½ × 11 inches or A4), you can put your name and address at the top, or just your name, or your initials. On the folded card, you might want to have your first name, your first and last names, your initials, or perhaps "A Note from Mary" (using your name, of course). And don't forget, you can have the words "Thank You," "An Invitation," or "It's a Party" printed on the card instead of your name, if you have a particular purpose in mind.

LETTERHEADS

A letterhead is a good place to start. Following are some possibilities.

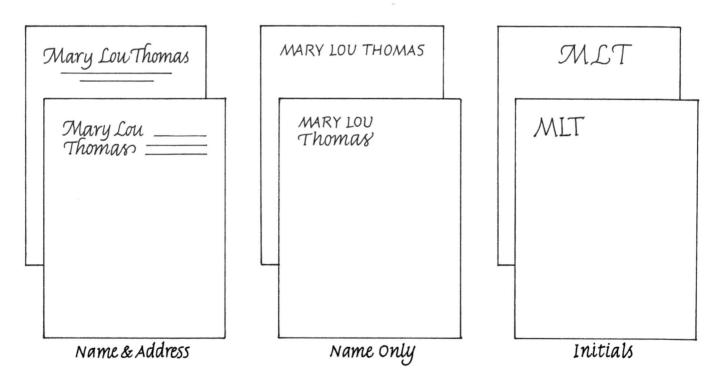

Name & Address   Name Only   Initials

Here are the decisions you need to make.

1. What words, letters, or initials do I want to use?
2. What style of calligraphy do I prefer?
3. How big or small do I want to write?

You can use more than one style of calligraphy or more than one size on the same piece of stationery, although that will make the process a bit more complicated.

Try several possibilities on practice paper. For example, if you want to use your whole name, write it in different sizes and different styles of calligraphy.

Then cut out all the versions you like and place them, one at a time, on a sheet of paper the size of the stationery. Try them in various positions—flush left, flush right, centered—to see how they look. You can also cut the first name and last name apart and put one above the other.

Once you have decided which version you prefer, write the words on a clean sheet of paper, in the same position as your chosen layout, using whichever pen or marker you used in your layout.

Be sure to use the correct guide lines for the alphabet and pen size. Also, unless you have a lot of money to spend, do the calligraphy in black, because color printing—in a copy shop—is much more expensive than printing in black. In most copy shops, you can find a selection of colored paper to print on. Your stationery can be bright and colorful even if the lettering is in black.

NOTE CARDS

Note cards can be designed and printed the same way as full-size stationery. Follow the same steps as you would for a letterhead. Decide what to write first, then try different versions of the same words or initials on practice paper.

Layout possibilities for inexpensive copy-machine printing can be chosen from these.

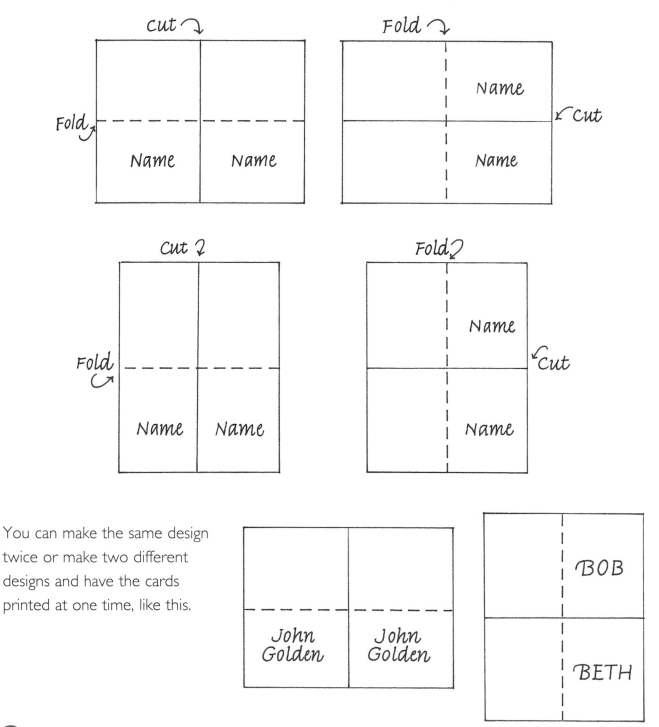

You can make the same design twice or make two different designs and have the cards printed at one time, like this.

After they are printed, cut the pages in half so that you get two cards out of one piece of paper. Some copy shops will do the cutting for you, or have a paper cutter that you can use. (If you've never used a paper cutter before, it's probably best to ask an adult to do the cutting for you.)

Hint If you are having note cards printed in a copy shop, you can have them copied on heavier paper than the normal copy-machine paper. Ask if they can show you samples of "heavier stock" or "cardstock." It will cost a little more than regular paper, but not too much. (Be sure to ask the price before you make your decision!)

"REAL" PRINTING

A print shop can also make your stationery for you, using a printing press to reproduce your calligraphy. If you go to a real printer (as opposed to a copy shop), your calligraphy can be printed in any color you like on a wide variety of papers. But the price will be much, much higher. It probably isn't worth it unless you have an uncle in the printing business.

17

Envelopes

*E*veryone loves to receive a beautifully handwritten envelope. Addressing envelopes is easy if you practice writing smaller with your 2-mm markers or fountain pens. In this chapter, you'll learn some formal and informal ways to address an envelope and how to make an envelope to match your handmade cards.

FORMAL ENVELOPES

One easy way to address an envelope is to put the guide lines inside it so that you can see them through the front of the envelope. If you are using a 2-mm marker or a wide fountain pen and want to write the address in Italic, you can use Guide Lines #2. With the narrower fountain pen, use Guide Lines #16.

Take these guide lines to a copy shop and have copies made on heavier paper (again, ask for cardstock). Then cut out the guide lines so that they are a little smaller than your envelopes. This way you can easily put them in the envelopes and remove them. The lines should be copied onto heavier paper so that the paper won't bend or tear when you put it into the envelopes or take it out.

If you are writing on a white envelope that doesn't have a decorative paper lining, you should be able to see the guide lines through the envelope well enough to write accurately.

If you can't see through the envelope, try this: Place your envelope over the guide lines, making sure that the lines are straight. If you like, use a small piece of removable tape to hold it in place, like this.

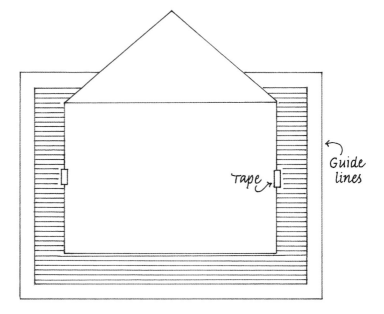

Hint If your envelopes are small, the 2-mm guide lines may be too big and the address won't fit on the envelope. Make copies of both the 2-mm and the smaller guide lines, just in case!

Use a ruler to connect the guide lines from the left side to the right side, making light pencil lines on your envelopes. Start about halfway down.

Hint It's much easier and more fun to address larger envelopes.

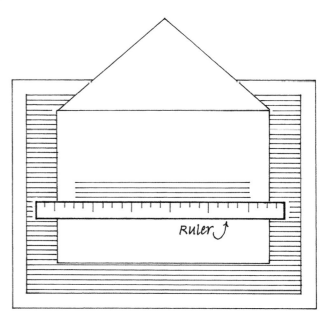

INFORMAL ENVELOPES

Start collecting blank envelopes. Look for shops that sell packages of envelopes in different colors. Sometimes they have too many of one color or size and sell them cheaply to get rid of them. Get larger ones if possible. Or just buy some inexpensive white envelopes in a stationery store or discount store that you can use for practicing (or fooling around).
Try some of these ideas.

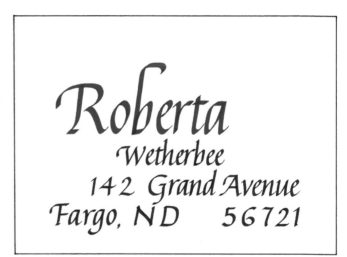

- Write the name larger (3.5-mm marker) and the address smaller.
- Use two or more colors—or even change colors—for each letter of the first name or last name.
- Write a formal envelope and decorate it with a border design, stickers, or rubber stamps.
- Try working without lines. If you write on a diagonal or let the lines or letters move up and down, it won't matter if they are uneven.
- Write the name with your calligraphy pen (or pens) and the address with a pointed marker or a gel pen, using Italic handwriting.

Hint If you are mailing these envelopes, as opposed to hand delivering them, be sure the address is easy to read. Otherwise, the post office may not deliver them!

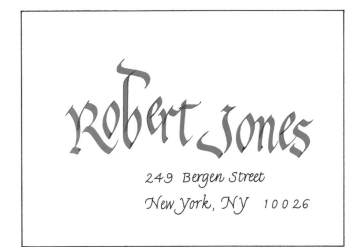

Making Cards to Fit Envelopes and Envelopes to Fit Cards

It's much easier to make a card that fits into an envelope than to find an envelope to match the size of the card, especially if the card is a funny size. But envelopes come in many different sizes and shapes. If you find some envelopes you like, you can cut out a card that's just a little smaller than the envelope so that it will fit. Remember that cards fold, so the actual size of the card is really a little smaller than *double* the size of the envelope.

On page 94 there are a few possibilities. These envelope sizes are usually easy to find.

If you are photocopying your cards or note cards in a copy shop, and the size of the folded card is based on a standard sheet of copy machine paper (unfolded size 8½ × 11 inches or A4), you should be able to find envelopes in any stationery store to fit your cards.

Hint
If you are looking for envelopes to match a card, bring the card with you to the stationery or art-supply store to see if they have something in the right size. It's easier than measuring the card and carrying your notebook and ruler with you!

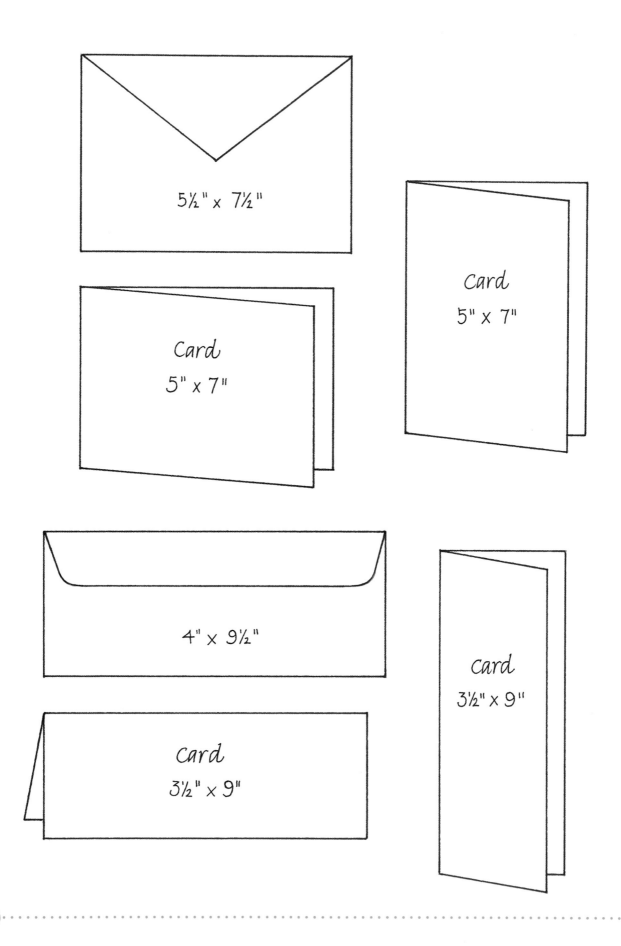

5½" x 7½"

Card
5" x 7"

Card
5" x 7"

4" x 9½"

Card
3½" x 9"

Card
3½" x 9"

Here's a simple method for making an envelope to fit a card that you already have. It has a lot of steps, but they should be pretty easy to follow.

1. Holding the card horizontally, cut out a piece of paper that is 1 inch (about 2.5 cm) wider than the card on each side and twice the height of the card plus 1 inch. Place the card on the paper a little above center.

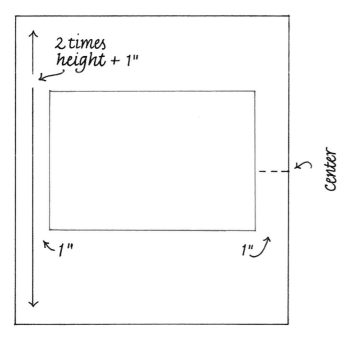

2. Fold the sides in, not quite touching the card.

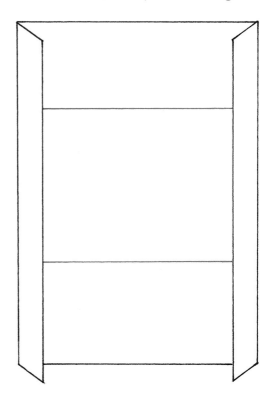

3. Fold the top and bottom over the card (also allowing a little "breathing space") with the top flap extending about 1 inch over the bottom flap.

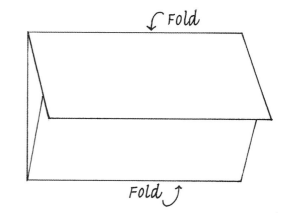

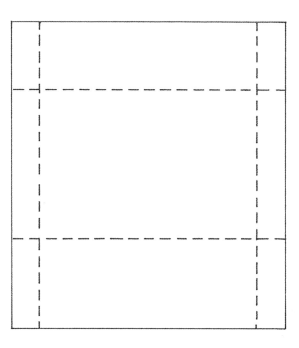

4. Open the piece of paper and take the card out. The paper should look like this. The dotted lines are fold lines.

5. Using scissors, cut out the four rectangles in the corners, following the creases.

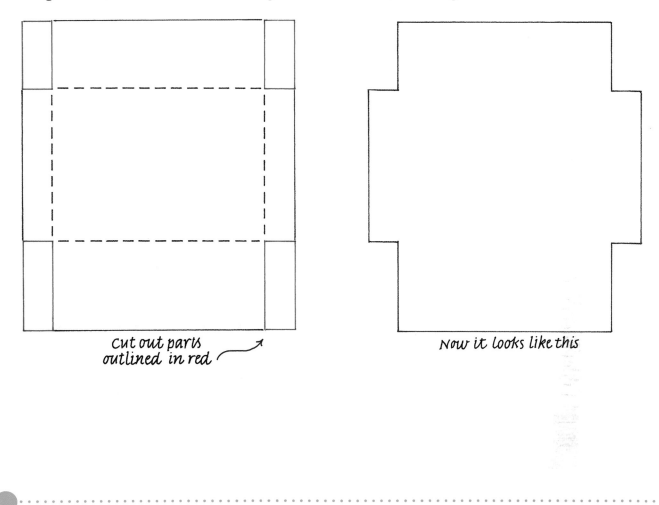

cut out parts
outlined in red ➚

Now it looks like this

6. Fold the sides in; then fold the bottom up and the top down. Measure about ¼ inch (0.6 cm) from each bottom edge of the top flap and make a pencil mark.

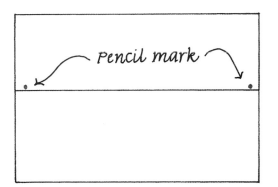

8. Make a pencil mark where the corners of the top flap meet the bottom flap. These marks will be on the bottom flap.

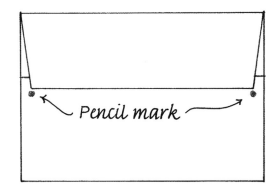

7. Draw a line from each pencil mark to the top corners and cut along the lines.

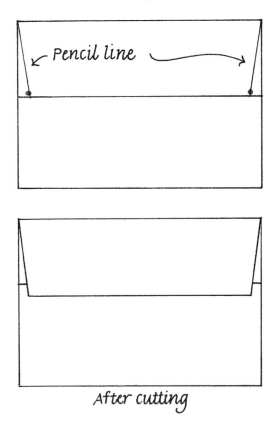

After cutting

9. Open the upper flap and draw a line from the bottom corners of the envelope through the pencil marks to the top of the bottom flap. Cut along those lines.

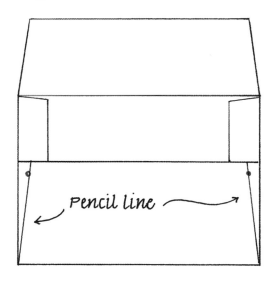

10. Your envelope will now look like this if you open all the folds.

11. Fold the side flaps in. Then fold the bottom flap up and glue it carefully to the side flaps. You can do this with a glue stick.

12. You can seal the envelope (after you put the card inside) with a little glue or with a sticker or colored tape.

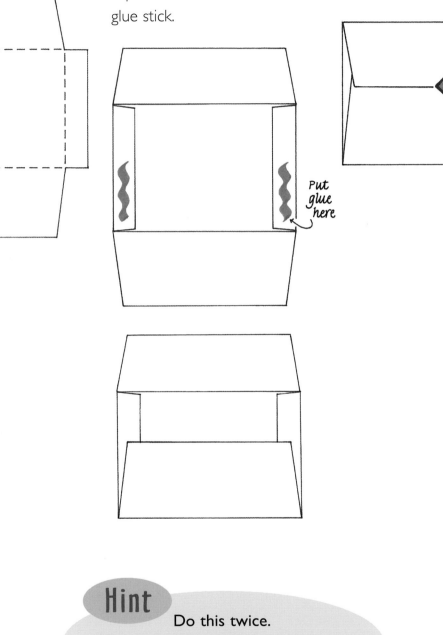

Put glue here

Hint

**Do this twice.
The second time will be much easier
than the first.**

18

Making Signs

*I*t's a lot of fun to make small signs to hang on your bedroom door or to put on your desk. Signs also make nice gifts. What would you put on a sign?

- your name or someone else's
- the name of a place, like "Alison's Room"
- information or a request: "Knock Before Entering," "Private," "Quiet Please," or "Party in Progress"
- a greeting, like "Happy Birthday" or "Welcome Home!"
- whatever message you like

What can you write on? Some heavy papers and certain kinds of cardboard are good for signs. Don't use thick gray cardboard because it will probably absorb the ink and not look very good.

Shiny cardboard, such as the kind gift boxes are made of, isn't very good to write on either.

One kind of heavy paper that's like thin cardboard is called Bristol board, or just Bristol. You can get a pad of it or buy it by the sheet at an art supply store. It's fairly inexpensive and can be cut with scissors or a paper cutter.

If you use Bristol, here's one important fact: There are two kinds (or surfaces) of Bristol available—very smooth and a little less smooth. The very smooth Bristol is called *plate,* and can be too slippery to write on. The other kind is called *medium* or *vellum Bristol* and is much easier to use. (If you ask for it in a shop, you have to say "vellum Bristol," not just "vellum," because vellum is another kind of material.)

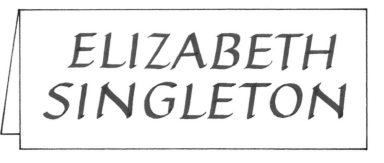

When making a sign, you will probably want to use the larger (3.5- or 5-mm) markers so that your letters will be large enough to read from a distance. It's OK to make a sign with smaller writing on it, but that would more likely be a very small sign, or maybe a folded sign to put on a desk. This is sometimes called a *tent card*.

Planning Your Sign

Here are some simple steps for making a sign to hang on a wall or door.

1. Decide what words you want to write and pick a calligraphy style.

2. Try sketching the sign a few different ways to find the best layout. For example, you can write the words on one line or two, centered, flush left, or flush right. Do this step using a pointed marker or a pencil. This is just to figure out how the words look, not to determine the actual measurements of the sign.

3. Choose the layout that looks best. Then, using your calligraphy pen, write the words carefully on your practice paper using the correct guide lines for the alphabet you have chosen. You may need to do this a few times until you are satisfied.

4. Draw lines around the words, leaving an inch or more (2 to 3 cm) all around so that the words have enough white space around them.

This will give you an idea of how the sign will look when it's finished and how big it will be.

5. On a piece of Bristol board or other heavy paper or cardboard, draw lines for your writing. Leave enough space around the words to cut the sign out after you finish the calligraphy. Try to make the lines the same distance apart and in the same position as on your practice paper. This isn't always easy to do!

Drawing Lines for Your Sign

Here's how you can make the lines on the sign match the lines on your practice paper.

1. Fold the sides of the practice paper like this.

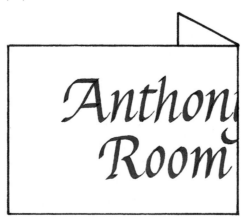

2. Then place this folded practice paper over your cardboard and make little pencil marks on the cardboard in the same position as the lines on the practice paper.

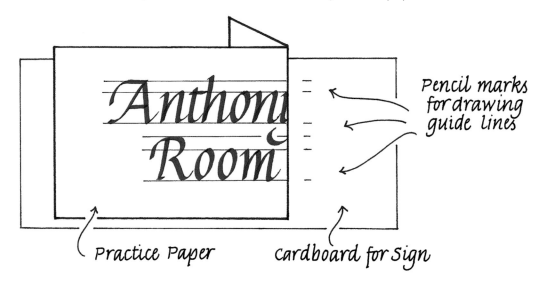

Pencil marks for drawing guide lines

Practice Paper

cardboard for sign

3. Do this on both the left and right sides of the cardboard so that you can connect the marks to draw your guide lines.

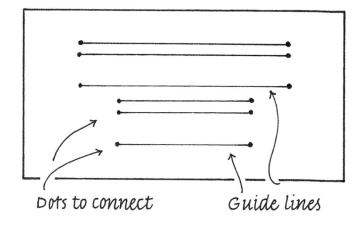

Dots to connect   Guide lines

You can do the same thing with a ruler by measuring the layout on the practice paper and making the same measurements on your cardboard before drawing the lines on it. Some people find this easy to do, but the folded paper method is probably easier.

After you have drawn the lines, you can do the calligraphy directly on the cardboard or Bristol. When the ink is dry, you can draw lines for the outside of the sign and cut it out.

Hint Another way to transfer the measurements from the practice layout to the cardboard (or Bristol) is to place the layout over a larger piece of cardboard. Making sure it is straight (not slanting uphill or downhill), use a ruler to extend the lines to the left and right from the layout to the cardboard. This is similar to the method used for drawing lines on envelopes in Chapter 17.

DECORATING YOUR SIGN

If you would like to make a border around your sign, it's always a good idea to do the border before cutting the sign out. That way, you can be sure you have enough space. A sign with a border will probably be a little bigger than one without a border.

You can decorate your sign in various ways. You could use some of these materials.

- metallic markers
- pointed colored markers
- rubber stamps
- stickers
- glitter
- painted decorations or photos

Another good idea is to mount the sign on a slightly larger piece of colored cardboard to create an "instant border." You can attach them with double-sided tape.

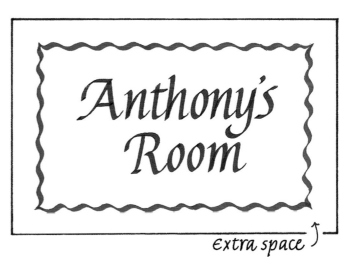

extra space

colored cardboard "instant border"

19

Calligrams

*C*alligrams are pictures made of words or letters. The word is the invention of a French poet, Guillaume Apollinaire. In the beginning of the twentieth century, he wrote poems that were printed in shapes or patterns. This is an example from Apollinaire's book, *Calligrammes*.

```
                    S
                    A
                   LUT
                    M
                 O     N
                    D
                    E
                  DONT
                 JE SUIS
                 LA LAN
                GUE   E
               LOQUEN
              TE  QUESA
             B O U C H E
            O    PARIS
            TIRE ET TIRERA
          T O U        JOURS
           AUX        A  L
         LEM            ANDS
```

Calligraphers have borrowed the term from Apollinaire and make their own calligrams using calligraphy. Here are two examples of calligrams made with calligraphy.

In the first example—using Monoline Italic and written with a gel pen—the outline of the star is made of letters with no other lines. This is probably the easiest way to begin to learn calligrams.

The apple calligram is solid. The calligraphy fills the entire shape of the apple, and was written with a calligraphy marker.

Calligrams are actually quite easy to make, although you'll need some time and patience. You are "allowed" to do a lot of things that aren't acceptable when doing some other kinds of projects. Your calligraphy doesn't even need to be very good to make a nice calligram.

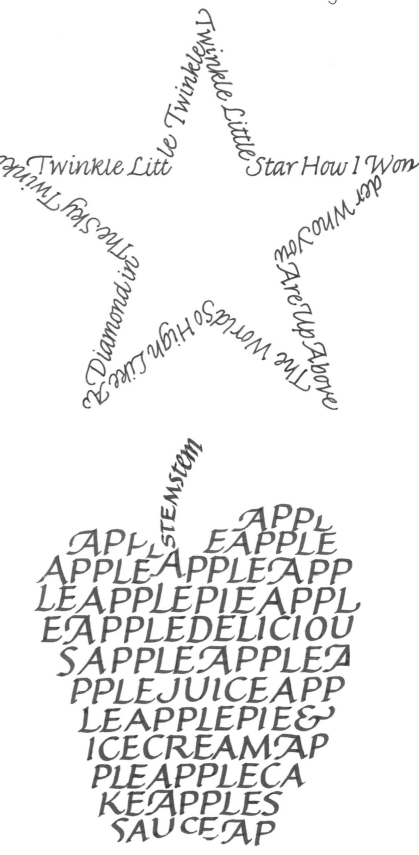

An Outline or Border-Design Calligram

Here are the steps for making a simple outline calligram.

1. Start by finding a pattern that you like. Here are several shapes that are easy to work with.

If you want to use one of these shapes, have this page photocopied in a copy shop. Have with the pictures you selected "blown up," that is, reproduced larger. Ask for them to be doubled in size (200%) or more.

Hint A simple shape is easier to work with than a more complicated one, especially for a beginner.

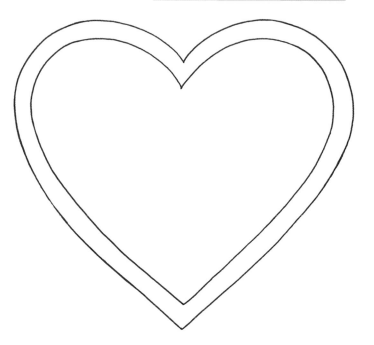

2. Put the pattern under a piece of practice paper, or any paper that you can see through, and lightly trace the outline in pencil. Then make a second line around the shape that's the distance—based on the pen or the marker you want to use—of the x-height (if you are using lowercase letters) or the capital height (if you are writing in capitals).

Hint If you make your double outline right on the pattern and put it under your paper, you won't have to make any pencil lines. Make the outline with a pointed black marker or a black ballpoint pen so you can see the lines clearly through the paper you'll be writing on. If you tape the pattern to the back of the practice paper (with small pieces of removable tape), the pattern will stay in place even when you move the paper. It's a good idea to make a few extra copies of the pattern in case you make a mistake or want to use different outlines.

A Few Suggestions

Simple letters, such as Italic simple capitals, Roman capitals, or Italic with shortened ascenders and descenders (Chapter 5), are easier (and faster!) to work with than more elaborate forms (like Gothic capitals).

You can also create your calligrams with gel pens, as in the star on page 105. Gel pens are easy to use, and some of the sparkly ones give you really nice results.

If you use a calligraphy pen or marker, the smaller the pen or marker size (which means the smaller the letters), the better the calligram will look. It will take more time than if you write large, but the shape will be clearer.

3. Write your calligraphy following the outline or border of the shape. Turn the paper as you go so that the pen or marker is always in the correct pen position. This is exactly the same procedure you'd follow if you were making an alphabet border. You may have to stop once in a while and wait for your ink to dry. That way you won't put your hand on the paper and smear the ink.

What letters or words should you use for your outline calligram?

■ a repeated message, like "I Love You" or "Happy Birthday"
■ a name, initials, or an alphabet
■ a line or two from a poem or quotation

4. If you've made any pencil lines on the calligram, you can either leave them or carefully erase them—allowing time for the ink to dry—using a kneaded eraser (available at any art-supply store).

Try to erase only the pencil lines without rubbing directly over the calligraphy to avoid smearing it.

A Filled-in or Solid Calligram

A filled-in calligram takes a little more time to make, but it has more possibilities.

1. Start the same way as with the outline calligram: Choose a pattern and, if it's too small, enlarge it in a copy shop. Trace it lightly on a piece of practice paper.

2. One way to fill it in is horizontally, by placing guide lines underneath and writing from left to right, starting and ending at the pencil outlines. Depending on the alphabet you choose and the size of the pen, this may give you a striped calligram. As you can see from this example, sometimes it is necessary to add a few extra lines to help make the shape more clear.

If you don't want so much white space between lines, try moving the guide lines after every line of writing so that your lines of calligraphy are closer together. This is easier to do if you write in capital letters than if you use minuscules with ascenders and descenders.

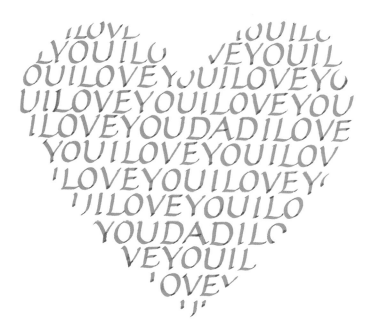

Notice how much easier it is to see the pattern if the lines of writing are closer together.

3. You can add a border to the shape by following the steps for an outline calligram.

Working Freely

It's also fun to make a calligram without using guide lines for the calligraphy. Here's how to do it.

1. Draw your pattern in pencil, or tape it underneath your paper.

2. Using your smaller markers or fountain pens, write in the space provided, estimating the size of the letters. You can also do this with a pointed marker or gel pen. Start along the inner edges of the shape so that you have a line to follow.

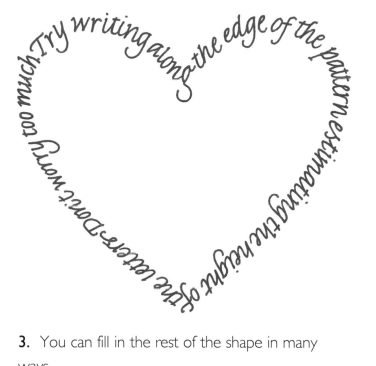

3. You can fill in the rest of the shape in many ways.

■ working around the outline and in toward the center
■ working across (without guide lines) and not worrying about each line being straight
■ changing pens or markers to make the letters in some parts bigger or smaller
■ using different colors or alphabets

It's also okay to add a few pen lines or some shading to help your shape become clearer.

When you write freely, you'll find that sometimes you need to stretch or squeeze the letters to make them fit into the pattern. That's okay as long as the letters aren't too distorted.

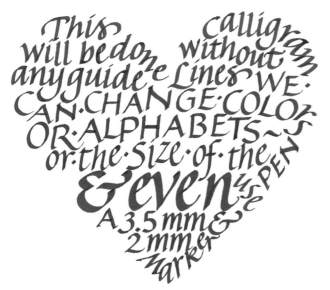

When you make a filled-in calligram, whether you use guide lines or write freely, you'll have lots more room for your message than when you make an outline calligram. You can write anything you like: a whole poem or quotation, a letter to a friend, a repeated name or message, any letters or words, or even numbers.

A CALLIGRAM CARD

1. Start by making a calligram that's fairly large, perhaps half the size of this page. Use black ink or a black marker.

2. Take it to a copy shop and have it reduced by half (ask for a 50% copy) or try different reductions. They don't cost much, so you can try a few different sizes. You'll be surprised to see how good your calligram will look (and how your mistakes won't show!) when it's smaller.

3. Cut out and glue your reduced calligram directly onto a blank greeting card, or have it printed to make a lot of cards. To do this, all you need is a sheet of paper 8½ × 11 inches (or A4) divided into quarters with lightly written pencil lines. Glue two calligrams into the spaces shown below. You can make either vertical or horizontal cards.

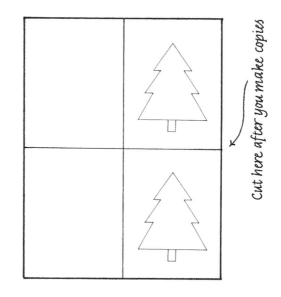

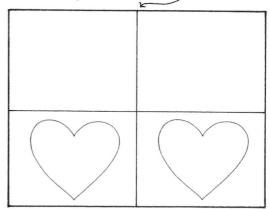

4. Now head back to the copy shop and have your glued design copied onto cardstock (heavier paper). Cut the copies in half (according to the diagram above) and fold them in half. You'll get two cards per page for very little money.

These cards will fit into standard-size envelopes.

Since the calligrams will come out in black, you can have them printed onto colored cardstock and then decorate them any way you like—with glitter or colored markers or metallic gel pens. Or don't decorate them at all; the calligram is already very artistic.

Write a personal message or sign your name on the inside and you'll have handmade holiday cards, birthday cards, or valentines.

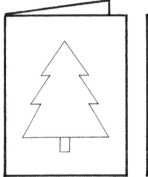  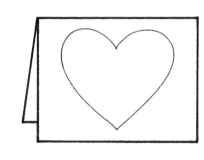 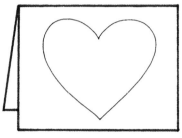

FINDING OTHER PATTERNS FOR CALLIGRAMS

You can make calligrams in all kinds of shapes. If you like to draw, you can make your own patterns. If you prefer, you can trace or photocopy shapes or pictures from lots of places. Children's books or coloring books, especially for very young children, often have a big variety of simple shapes or pictures.

You can also find advertisements in magazines or pictures on greeting cards or gift wrap that are easy to photocopy. Just remember that you'll generally need to get larger photocopies. If you make a tracing of a drawing or photo, you only need to trace the outline or the most important lines to make your calligram patterns.

20

Using "Real" Pens

Having come this far in your study of calligraphy, you have probably tried writing with quite a few different tools.

- pencils
- pointed markers
- wide, medium, and narrow calligraphy markers
- wide and narrow fountain pens
- double pencils

But by now you are certainly aware that calligraphy is also done with dip pens and ink. It's a joke to call them "real" pens—all the pens you've been using are real. But writing with a pen that has been dipped into ink is a wonderful experience for any calligrapher.

In the past, pens were made of feathers from either turkeys or geese. These pens are called *quills,* and many calligraphers who work in traditional ways still make and use their own quills.

NIBS AND PENHOLDERS

Dip pens generally consist of steel nibs (pen points) that fit into separate penholders. They are also called *broad-edged nibs.*

You can buy these broad-edged nibs in many art-supply stores or from mail-order calligraphy dealers. Popular brands include Mitchell, Brause, Speedball, and Tape, and they are available for both right-handed and left-handed calligraphers.

Penholders made of plastic or wood are available in just about any art-supply store.

Just like calligraphy markers, dip pen nibs come in many different widths, from very narrow to quite wide. In fact, you should be able to find a wider variety of nib sizes for dip pens than for markers or fountain pens.

If you use Brause or Tape nibs, the width of the nib is measured in

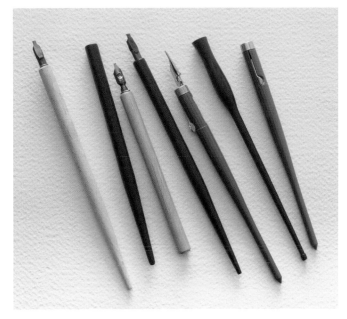

Penholders for calligraphy nibs.

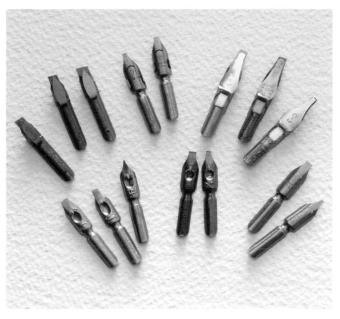

Nibs come in many sizes.

millimeters (just like your markers) and is visible right on the nib. Mitchell and Speedball nibs are numbered differently—the nibs with the lowest numbers (such as a Mitchell #0 or 1, or a Speedball C-0 or C-1) are the widest, and the higher numbers are smaller. These numbers don't give you the measurement of the nib.

INK

Unlike fountain pens, which generally use ink cartridges, you'll need to get a bottle of ink to use with dip pens. There are lots of different kinds of ink available, and they come in many different colors.

But here's the most important thing to remember: **Don't buy waterproof ink. Use nonwaterproof ink for calligraphy.** Waterproof inks will spoil your nibs and make your calligraphy look bad. (The thin lines come out too thick and the edges of the thick strokes appear lumpy.) Most inks labeled "India ink" are waterproof.

Some of the nonwaterproof ink brands are Parker, Waterman, Pelikan, and Quink fountain pen inks; Higgins Eternal; and some special calligraphy inks, such as Pearlescent.

TIPS FOR WORKING WITH PEN AND INK

1. Tape your ink bottle to the table with masking tape so that it won't spill if you bump into it.

2. After you dip your pen into the ink, press it lightly against the inside edge of the bottle to allow the excess ink to drip back into the bottle. Then start the pen by making a few lines

on a scratch sheet (a small piece of the same paper you will be writing on) to get the ink flowing before you write on your real paper. This will prevent blobs.

3. Keep a container of water next to your ink so you can rinse off your pen occasionally. Dry the nib on a paper towel or a soft cloth before dipping it into your ink again. Also do this when you stop writing. The nib will work better if you clean it pretty regularly.

4. Use the same guide lines that you use for markers or fountain pens of the same width as your dip pens.

5. The edge of a dip pen is sharper than a marker or a fountain pen, so it's harder to

make strokes going backward. Dip pens work better from top to bottom and from left to right than from bottom to top or right to left. For some letters that you normally make in one stroke (with a marker or fountain pen), you may need two or three strokes with a dip pen, especially when you use the widest nibs. Below is the Italic **a** and **g,** written first with a marker and then with a dip pen.

6. You'll probably have to write more slowly with dip pens, but your letters will come out blacker (if you use black ink) and richer looking, and the thin lines will be thinner.

Working with dip pens isn't as easy as writing with markers or fountain pens, but it's definitely worth the effort.

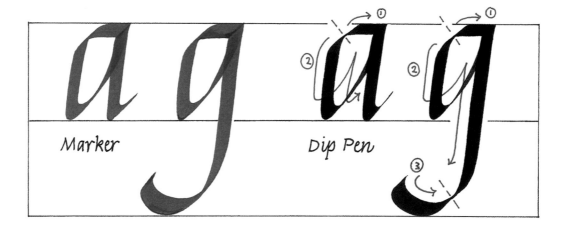

Marker   Dip Pen

GUIDE LINES

#1 Basic Italic

Use with 3.5-mm markers.

#2 Basic Italic

Use with 2-mm markers or with B or B-3 fountain pens.

#3 Italic Variations

Use with 3.5-mm markers.

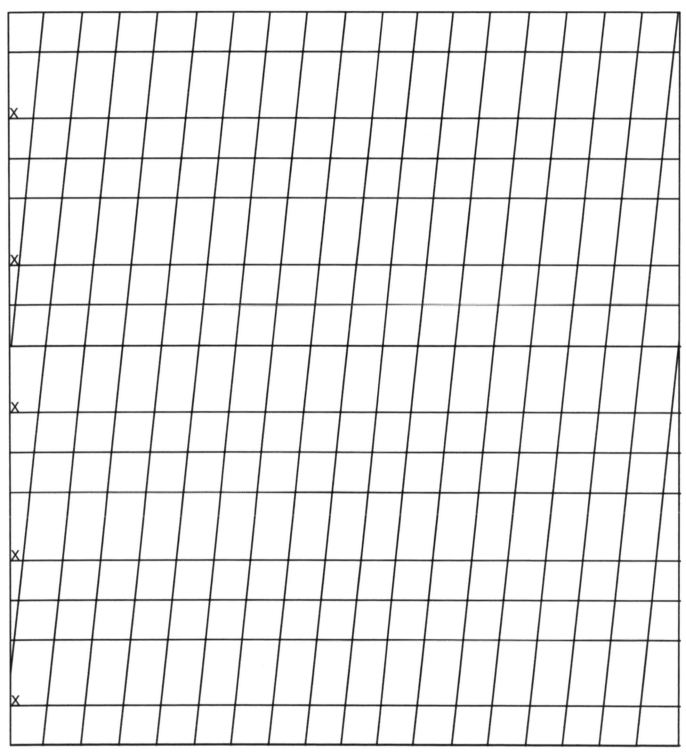

Guide Lines

#4 Italic Variations

Use with 3.5-mm markers.

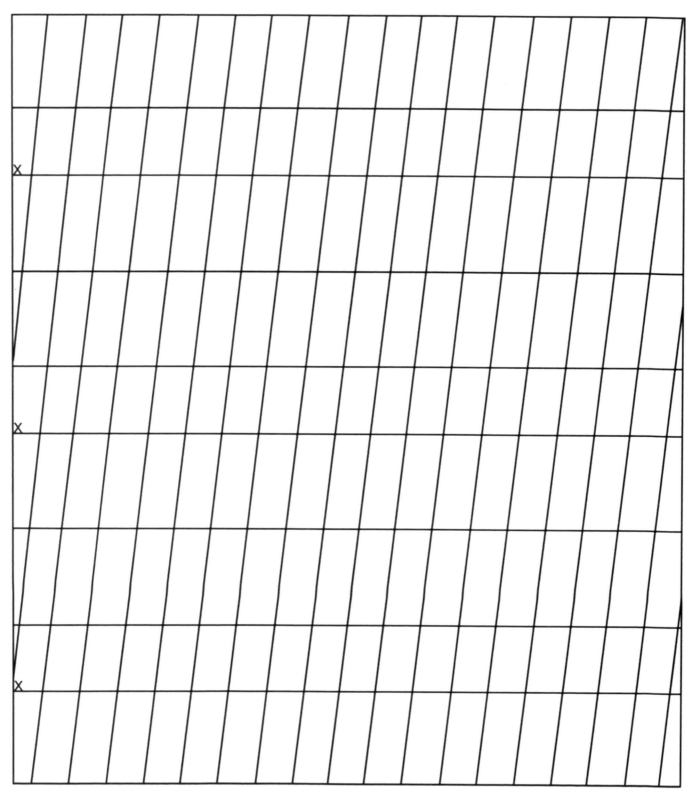

#5A Italic Variations

Use with 2-mm markers or with B or B-3 fountain pens.

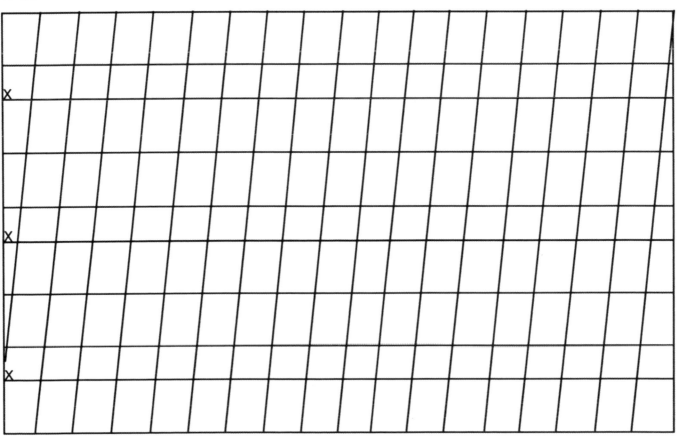

#5B

#6 Italic Variations

Use with 3.5-mm markers.

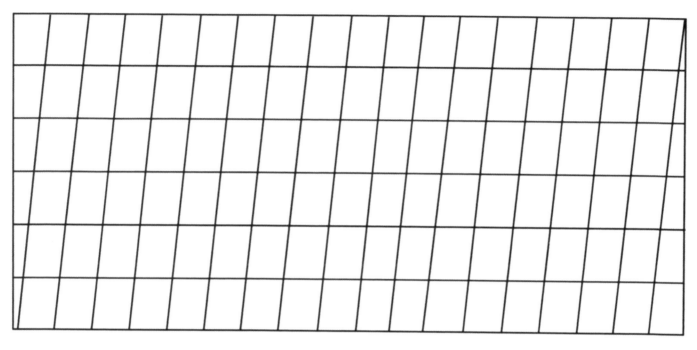

#7 Italic Variations

Use with 3.5-mm markers.

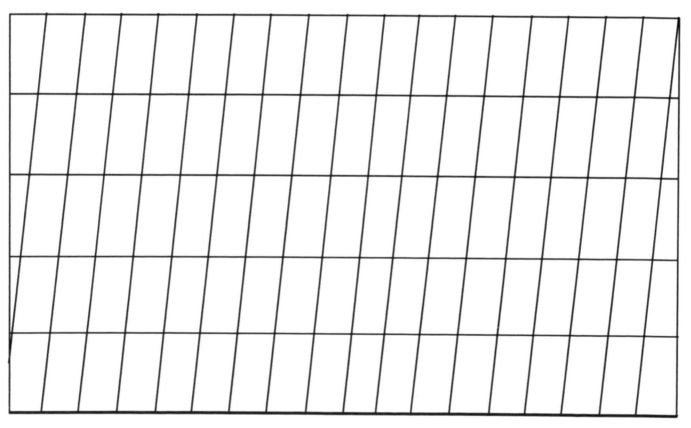

#8A Italic Variations

Use with 2-mm markers or with B or B-3 fountain pens.

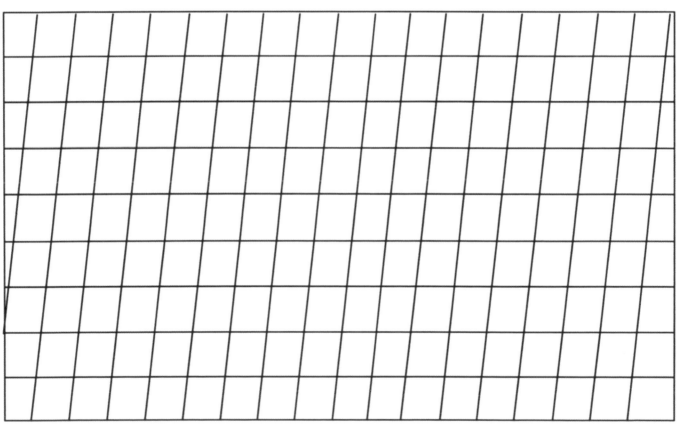

#8B

#9 Textura and Swing Gothic

Use with 3.5-mm markers.

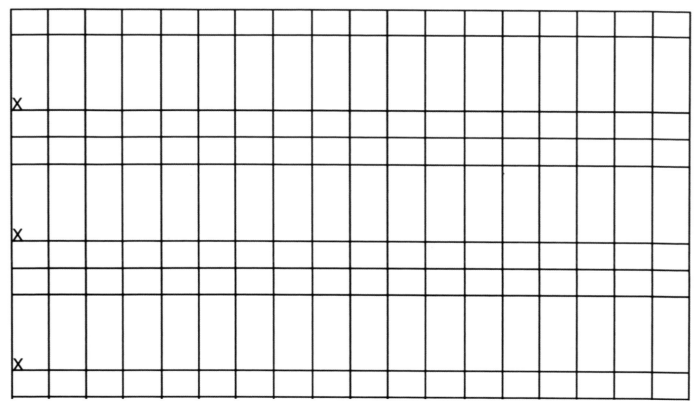

#10 Textura and Swing Gothic

Use with 2-mm markers or with B and B-3 fountain pens.

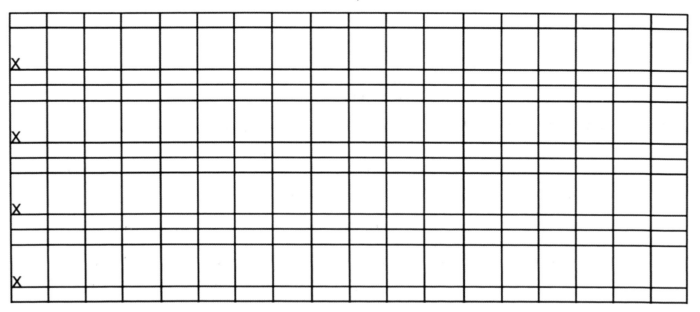

#11 Modern Gothic

Use with 3.5-mm markers.

#12 Modern Gothic

Use with 2-mm markers or with B or B-3 fountain pens.

#13 Italic   Writing Larger

Use with 5-mm markers.

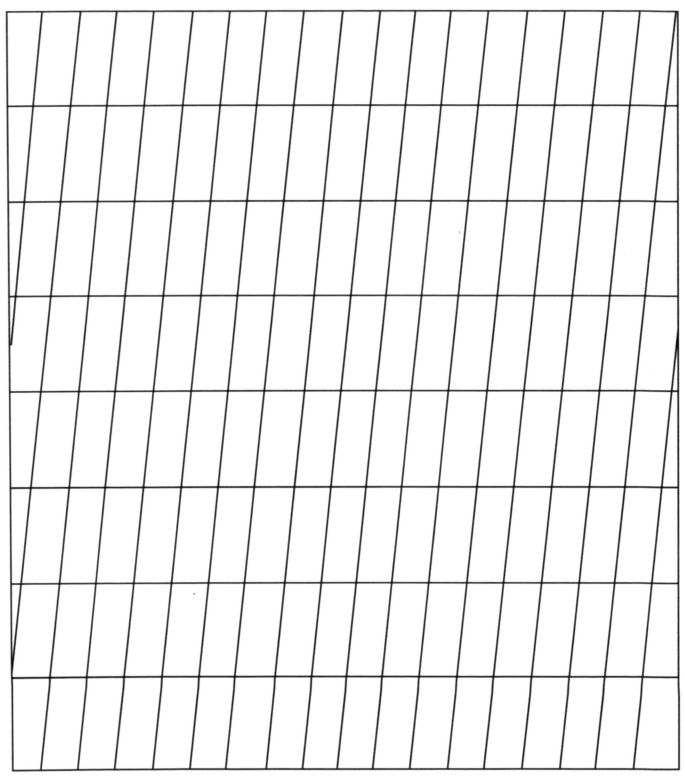

#14 Textura or Swing Gothic Writing Larger

Use with 5-mm markers.

#15 Modern Gothic Writing Larger

Use with 5-mm markers.

#16 Italic Writing Smaller

Use with medium (M) fountain pens.

Index